PIZZA DE LUXE

For Izzi and Gigi

STEFANO MANFREDI

PIZZA DE LUXE

Deliciously authentic recipes for the world's favourite fast food

MURDOCH BOOKS

SYDNEY · LONDON

CONTENTS

New wave – new pizza

Pizza is probably the world's most popular fast food and wherever it has gone, it has taken on the characteristics of its new home. While Italy, and more precisely Naples, is where it all began, there's no doubt that pizza now belongs to the world. But something exciting is happening in pizza's spiritual home. What I call the 'new wave' of pizza has been gaining momentum in Italy in the last decade and that inspiring movement is the focus of this book.

I've been researching pizza in Italy for many years now and I've noticed a huge change in the way it is made at every step of the process. It has been led by chefs/pizzaioli whose curiosity and eye for quality has led them back to the fundamental building blocks of pizza-making, from the growing of the grain and the milling process to temperatures, fermentation and maturation times for the dough.

Where has this change in pizza-making led us? Much like the recent movement away from industrial white bread towards artisan loaves with natural leavening and specialist flours, it's a look back as well as a step forward. 'New wave' pizza-making is a movement that returns to pizza's origins before industrial flour milling, while at the same time using modern advances in stone milling, machinery and oven technologies.

This step forward in pizza-making has by necessity taken place outside Naples. If you look closely at pizza kitchens in Naples you'll find that many of them use highly refined '00' flour, as outlined by one of the groups set up to standardise Naples-style pizza. This flour is relatively cheap, has had the wheat bran and germ removed in the refining process and has the consistency of talcum powder. Now, there is nothing wrong with this and the use of '00' flour more or less defines the 'Naples-style' pizza as we know it today, but what happens when you use different flours, milled with stone and free of these strictures? What can be achieved when these flours are then used with different types of fermentation procedures? These are some of the questions we will look at in this book.

After all, even when pizza appeared in Naples in the first half of the eighteenth century, it would be over a century before the modern roller mill was invented. So, for at least a hundred years, stone-milled flour was used to make pizza. Granted, the bran was partly sifted out by pizzaioli even back then, but the grain was milled in its entirety, and this is fundamental to its structure. The roller mill brought us white flour. White flour meant uniformity, consistency and less technical ability needed on the part of the pizzaioli. As well, this flour lasts a long time and can therefore be exported and used to make a similar quality product around the world.

The other feature of 'new wave' pizza is the focus on quality ingredients to go on top. With the exponential spread of pizza post World War II and, more recently, globalisation, this fast food has become 'devalued'. In Italy, the margin on a typical pizza is so small that many of the pizzerie have developed a way to use cheap flour, short fermentation and maturation times, and poor ingredients to remain profitable. Now, not everyone adheres to these minimums, but with price pressures dictated by the market, the fact that stoneground flour costs more and that long, 'indirect' fermentation methods take longer to make and are more involved, there is an incentive to take the easiest route. This approach is not just limited to Italy. As the pizza of Italy, and Naples in particular, is seen worldwide as a benchmark, the world for the most part follows.

This book will take the reader through what we do at my pizzeria, Pizzaperta Manfredi in Sydney, Australia. I have been a chef, running restaurants of the highest quality, for over 30 years. I have studied the methods and procedures of some of the protagonists of the 'new wave' pizza movement in Italy and this book is the result.

My hope is that the information here will guide home cooks and professionals alike to explore the possibilities of pizza-making and to take pizza back to what it once was – a healthy and delicious fast food.

STEFANO MANFREDI

What is pizza?

Pizza is a descendant of flatbread, the world's most ancient bread. People starting making flatbread as soon as they learnt to grind grain, mix it with water, then cook it on hot stones, a griddle or in a makeshift oven. Whether it was made from corn, rice, potato, wheat, yam or another farinaceous edible plant, the flatbread sprang up in various parts of the world as people had the same idea. It was the first bread and it not only helped to hold other foods, but could be carried around and stored easily as a delicious snack or meal.

It appears that the version of pizza we know today – the round, puffy-bordered, wood-fired type – was born in Naples and was mostly confined to that city for over 200 years, as were the specialist pizzerie and pizzaioli who made pizza, along with the development of the special ovens that cooked it. In 1884, in her book *Il Ventre di Napoli*, Matilde Serao describes an attempt to open a pizzeria in Rome, just 200 kilometres (125 miles) to the north of Naples. It was a novelty for a while, but it ended badly, with the entrepreneur going broke. Sophisticated Rome looked down on this street food from the south.

The two centuries of isolation were essential for the refinement of pizza in Naples, which at the time was one of the most populous cities in Europe. Back then Naples was not the sprawling city it is today. It was confined to a much smaller area, and was one of the most densely populated and poorest cities on the continent. People lived in small rooms in buildings of up to seven storeys, a contrast to other European cities of the time whose buildings were, at most, half as high. Cooking was difficult and dangerous in these cramped conditions. A visit to the old part of the city today will attest to the narrow lanes and the density of the housing.

Pizza developed in these densely populated streets as a cheap fast food, sold by the slice from stalls set up right on the laneways where half a million people were crammed into an area a tenth the size of today's Naples. The refinement of this popular food was not only driven by the intensely competitive market of the city's streets, but also by the character of Neapolitans themselves. Antonio Mattozzi writes in his book *Inventing the Pizzeria – A History of Pizza Making in Naples*:

Barrels of ink have been spilled describing the character of the Neapolitan. The marvellous natural setting, the fabulous blue sky, pleasing weather, and exceptional panoramas juxtaposed with the daily struggle for survival under difficult (albeit negotiable) conditions made the Neapolitan a cunning dreamer, romantic but pragmatic, kind and violent, but enormously creative. Imagination and creativity were lavished on the invention of new trades. One stood out for being so widespread: that of the pizzaiolo and the pizzeria.

Ingredients

I need to know the history of a food. I need to know where it comes from.
I have to imagine the hands that have grown, worked and cooked what I eat.

Carlo Petrini, Founder of the Slow Food Movement

In the more than 30 years that I've been in charge of restaurants, one of my most critical jobs has been to find the right ingredients. Perhaps it was the way I was brought up. My father always had a vegetable garden and a variety of fruit trees such as fig, apricot, peach, lemon and mulberry. He would bring sacks and boxes full of freshly picked fruits and vegetables to our restaurants. Even now, I'm obsessed with where ingredients come from and who grows, makes or fishes them. It should be no different with what goes into and onto a pizza.

It is fundamental for me to understand the ingredients I use in my restaurants by getting to know the territory and people who produce them. For me, visiting these producers as regularly as possible is crucial. For example, we use stoneground flours from Petra and Mulino Marino in Italy and some local flours from stone mills in Australia. I have visited both the Italian mills and I'm in the process of establishing relationships with the Australian mills. I've also visited our olive oil suppliers, Frantoio Franci in Montenero d'Orcia, Tuscany and Frantoio Cutrera in Chiaramonti Gulfi, Sicily.

Sometimes it's about finding one of the definitive producers of an ingredient in Italy so that I know what to look for in a locally made one. Australia has strict quarantine laws and prohibits the entry of a number of key ingredients,

such as Italian salami, coppa and unpasteurised soft cheeses. I've always travelled back to the source, the origin, to taste the ingredient as it has evolved in its own birthplace, its own territory, before choosing local ingredients.

For the dough

FLOURS

Flour is the starting point for making pizza. For too long it has been overlooked as a sort of given of our industrial age. As has been the case with so many of the foods we take for granted in this way, some of the more curious among us have reviewed how we produce what we eat and drink and, with a greater understanding, have tried to use technology to create something special.

There has been a revival of interest in artisan bread-making in the new world countries over the past decades. It runs along the same lines as wine, beer, salt and even sugar, whose producers have been looking carefully at what has been lost or removed in the industrial process that can contribute to flavour, texture, look, feel and general well-being for the consumer. Pizza is now having its turn and flour is where we have to start.

Flour can be made from many ingredients: rice, corn, rye, buckwheat, lentils, beans, potato, chia, amaranth, teff, chestnut and so on. But flour milled from wheat is the most commonly used throughout the world, especially in bread and pizza, because it contains a large amount of gluten.

Gluten is a composite of the proteins gliadin and glutenin. These are present, along with starch, in the endosperm of wheat. Gliadin allows dough to be malleable and stretchy, while glutenin makes it tough and resilient. Gluten is also present in rye and barley flours, but in much smaller amounts. These two proteins make up around 80 per cent of the total protein in wheat berries and it is primarily the proteins in gluten that give wheat dough its wonderful elasticity and structure.

The wheat berry is made up of three basic parts once the husk (or hull) has been removed:

BRAN / The bran is the outside layer of the wheat berry and accounts for roughly 15 per cent of its weight. It is made up of soluble and insoluble dietary fibre, mineral salts and vitamins.

ENDOSPERM / This forms the largest part of the wheat berry, accounting for around 83 per cent of its total weight. It contains protein, sugar, carbohydrates, iron and soluble fibre.

GERM / The germ is the embryo of the wheat berry. It's the part that will germinate to form a new plant. It is the smallest part of the berry, making up 2 per cent of its weight. It is rich in oils and gives flour a 'nutty' flavour and perfume. It is also important because it contains complex B vitamins. In refined flours it is absent because these oils, or fats, inhibit very long storage times.

If you've made bread or pizza before, you will have noticed that when dough is worked properly it can be stretched thinly, almost like bubble gum. It's this ability to form an elastic structure within the dough that traps the carbon dioxide produced by fermentation. And it is these small carbon dioxide bubbles that make the dough rise. Once the dough is baked, these bubbles remain as holes (alveoli), giving the bread or pizza its texture. The size of the bubbles, the softness of the dough and the crispness or firmness of the crust can be controlled through a number of techniques, which will all be discussed later.

Wholemeal and whole-wheat flours

Also called **wholegrain** flour, **wholemeal** has been milled using the whole-wheat kernel. That is the bran, endosperm and germ.

To make **whole-wheat** flour the bran, endosperm and germ are separated and milled. The flour made with the endosperm then has proportions of bran and germ added back, depending on the sort of flour needed. With stoneground whole-wheat flour, varying portions of the outside bran layer can be removed before milling to give the desired results. It will have more or less colour depending on the amount of bran the flour contains.

The flours we use are **whole-wheat** (rather than wholemeal) and contain varying degrees of bran and the entire germ. Because they are stone-milled and not bleached, they are darker and a little coarser than other commercial flours. This will result in a pizza with a crust that's also a little darker, but more fragrant and tasty.

It is important that you find flours that work well for you. This will mean doing research and perhaps contacting mills or flour companies for details. It's not that difficult. I've found milling companies on the whole are more than happy to communicate with clients who want to know more about their flours. It will also mean experimenting with different flours.

Modern industrial roller-milled white flours are made up almost entirely of the endosperm, removing both bran and germ. Their appearance is uniformly white. But industrial doesn't always mean 'bad'. It denotes a repetitive process with consistent results, nothing more, nothing less. There are many pizza-makers creating outstanding pizza with roller-milled flour. But there is a whole new world of pizza-making that can be explored with flours containing various degrees of bran and germ.

Flour classification

There's a great confusion about the way Italy classifies its flour. The majority of pizza dough recipes call for '00' flour and, given its prevalence in the Naples-style pizza, the home enthusiast and professional alike often believe this flour is 'the best'.

But what does '00' mean? And what of the other grades of flour? At the most basic level the numbers are a classification of how fine or coarse a flour is milled, '00' being the finest and, in increasing coarseness, '0', '1', '2' and finally *integrale*, or wholemeal. With each grade there is a corresponding minimum percentage of protein allowed – the finer the grade, the lower the allowed minimum. Because it's a minimum allowed, it means in theory that across types of soft wheats, grown in different microclimates, it's possible for a '00' and '0' grade to have elevated protein contents, but it's much easier for the coarser grades because they contain more of the bran and germ, where extra protein can be recovered.

We tend to use types '1', '2' and *integrale* flours in our pizze and blend them when we need different results. These grades are naturally obtained in the stone-milling process.

In the roller-milling process, the germ and bran are removed and white 'plain' or '00' and '0' flour are made using the endosperm. The bran and germ are processed separately and added back to the white flour in various quantities. Because stone mills produce flour from the entire grain, it retains much of its protein content, rich in fibre and gluten, though there may, as mentioned earlier, be some of the outer bran layer removed prior to milling.

The other important measurement that we look for in flour is its 'working gluten strength' or W quotient. It's a numerical value that measures tenacity against extensibility of flour when mixed with water in dough. The higher the number, the more hydration (water) it can absorb and it can take a more complex and longer fermentation and maturation. This is a general W strength guide:

WEAK FLOURS / Up to W 170, these flours absorb around 50 per cent of their weight in water. These flours are used for biscuits, cakes and grissini.

MEDIUM FLOURS / From W 180 to W 260, these flours absorb up to 65 per cent of their weight in water. For direct fermentation doughs, olive oil-based breads and focacce.

STRONG FLOURS / From W 280 to W 370, these flours absorb up to 75 per cent of their weight in water. Used for indirect and natural fermentation doughs, sourdough breads and where long fermentation and maturation times are necessary.

There are also very strong flours with quotients of W 400 and these can absorb 100 per cent and more of their weight in water.

Note that if in your part of the world you cannot find stone-milled flours, then you need to look for a 'bread' or 'high gluten' flour.

All flour is perishable and should not be kept for more than 3–4 months. Store in a sealed container or bag in a cool, dry place, preferably at around 18°C (64°F).

The wheat family

All the wheat species we have today belong to the genus *Triticum*. It is generally understood that the domestication of wheat species dates back to the Fertile Crescent (the ancient lands that ran along the Nile, Tigris and Euphrates rivers) around 10,000 years ago. The first domesticated wheat species were einkorn (*Triticum monococcum*) and emmer (*Triticum dicoccum*).

With domestication came thousands of years of selection by farmers and industry all over the world, which resulted in the species *Triticum aestivum*, our common 'soft' bread flour wheat, being the most planted type today.

Mention also needs to be made of spelt (*Triticum spelta*). Together with einkorn and emmer, these three species are considered the grandparents of modern wheat. In Italy, depending on the area, the word 'farro' can mean any one of these. The three species are similarly confused in other parts of the world, so when buying spelt, emmer or einkorn flour it is always advisable to look for the Latin names.

The second most cultivated wheat species is the 'hard' wheat *Triticum durum*, its cultivars used for dried pasta and bread, as well as certain types of pizze and focacce.

Another of the 'hard' species Khorasan (*Triticum turanicum*) and its sub-species Kamut are increasingly being used in pizza- and bread-making because of their high protein content and flavoursome results.

Rye (*Secale cereale*) is related to wheat and can be very useful in small percentages to give a dough a particular nuance in flavour. Rye flour is high in gliadin but low in glutenin and, because of this, it has a lower gluten content in comparison with wheat flours.

Once you have mastered the basic dough recipes in this book, you might like to experiment by substituting some of these species in small percentages.

WATER

When water is mixed with flour the proteins contained in flour are activated and transformed into gluten, which gives the resulting dough its viscosity and elasticity.

The mesh that's formed through this action is dependent on the quality and quantity of proteins in the flour and this net traps the gases formed during fermentation. These trapped gasses are the reason the dough rises and bubbles.

The water used has to be of a certain quality for optimum results. It can't contain too many mineral salts as they inhibit leavening and chlorine can kill enzymes. To mitigate against this, we use a filter, which renders the water relatively free of these impurities.

Shop-bought bottled water can be used as a last resort. The water should be still, not sparkling, is best from glass bottles, and a check on the label will give the water's pH levels. Ideally, water should have a pH between 5 and 6. Testing kits can be bought online or in hardware or specialist shops. You should not use tap water as it contains chlorine.

YEAST

Yeast is made up of a group of single-celled organisms, primarily *Saccharomyces cerevisiae*, which belong to the fungi kingdom. Together with flour and water, the addition of yeast initiates the crucial fermentation phase of dough. Yeast feeds on sugars contained in flour, producing carbon dioxide and alcohol, which allow the dough to rise. There are two types that can be used:

COMMERCIAL YEAST / This comes in two types. Firstly as a 'fresh' compressed cake, which can be bought occasionally from specialist food stores. When I first began making pizza, this was what I used. It's highly inconsistent as it degrades with time.

Better to use is dried or instant powdered yeast, which activates when it comes in contact with water. The best results are obtained if the dried yeast is mixed with a small quantity of water before being added to the flour and more water to make the dough.

NATURAL YEAST / This is made by mixing flour and water and allowing bacteria from the air to ferment it. The resulting yeast contains *Saccharomyces* as well as lactic and acetic acids. It's commonly known as a 'sourdough starter' or, in Italian, *lievito madre* (mother yeast). Making pizza using your own yeast is very satisfying, though it does take some daily maintenance. The yeast needs to be fed regularly and kept at constant temperatures.

There are two distinct types of natural starters: a runny, liquid type and a solid type. The difference is primarily in the hydration or water content. In Italy, it's the solid type that is used more in pizza-making because it is easier to regulate hydration. There are many methods for making a sourdough starter and those who wish to pursue this advanced method should substitute natural for dried or fresh yeast in the recipes at a ratio of up to 25 per cent sourdough for every kilogram of flour used.

There's no argument that natural yeast gives a different result to your pizza dough. But it takes time to prepare and time to maintain. Commercial yeast will give you more certainty and consistency across the whole year. Both types of yeasts have their place.

SALT

Salt not only brings out the flavour in dough – in much the same way as it seasons food – but also limits it from rising too quickly. If it rises too quickly, the yeast will expire before it has done its work.

Salt also acts as a preservative, stops the proliferation of unwanted bacteria and slows the formation of lactic acid. As well, it helps regulate the uniformity of the alveoli in the cooked dough.

When making dough it's important to always add the salt after mixing the yeast, water and flour. These last three need to react and bind. Adding salt in this phase will inhibit the process.

I use a natural sea salt for making my pizza.

EXTRA VIRGIN OLIVE OIL

Extra virgin olive oil is a fat but, unlike most other oils or fats, it has not been heated or chemically extracted. This means that it retains all its beneficial compounds and aromatic structure. Extra virgin olive oil acts to soften and flavour pizza dough but, like all other ingredients, it must be of good quality.

Extra virgin olive oil is used in dough to a maximum of 5 per cent of the weight of the flour. As well, extra virgin olive oil is used to drizzle onto the finished pizza.

Pizza doughs

In this section I set out the methods for making pizza doughs. Firstly there are the round, Naples-style pizza doughs and then the Roman-style doughs, cooked in a rectangular tray.

You'll notice that there is no use of the Neapolitan-preferred '00' flour here. 'New pizza' is about exploring ingredients and the most fundamental is the grain that makes up the flour. Some pizzaioli go to great lengths in this regard, sourcing their own wheat and having it milled to their specifications. Yes, it's obsessive and geeky, but no more obsessive than growing your own produce if you have a restaurant.

The recipes here begin with simple procedures – when you feel confident, you can move on to the more complex. It's a matter of finding the method that works for you.

Basic pizza dough / Direct method

The direct method for producing pizza dough is the easiest because all the ingredients are mixed together at about the same time. This is the method that the large majority of pizza-makers use because it's simple and quick.

For our recipes, however, we extend the maturation phase of the dough in the refrigerator so the final cooked pizza is easily digested and the flavour of the wheat maximised. Using an unrefined, stoneground whole-wheat (not wholemeal) flour is important because of its rich nutrients and the fact that it means less yeast is needed for fermentation and the maturation phase is thus more effective.

Fresh yeast dough

This recipe is for making pizza using 'fresh' or compressed yeast. Each 250 g (9 oz) ball of dough will make one 30 cm (12 inch) pizza, which feeds one person.

1 kg (2 lb 4 oz/6⅔ cups) unbleached, stoneground whole-wheat flour or strong bread flour
550 ml (19 fl oz) water at room temperature
8 g (¼ oz) fresh (compressed) yeast
20 g (¾ oz) sea salt
30 ml (1 fl oz) extra virgin olive oil

Place the flour and 500 ml (17 fl oz/2 cups) of the water in a mixer fitted with a dough hook attachment. Begin mixing on a low speed and keep mixing until the flour has absorbed all the water but is still not smooth. This should take only 3–4 minutes. Stop the mixer and let the dough rest in the bowl for 15–20 minutes.

Meanwhile, dissolve the yeast in the remaining water. Once the dough has rested, turn the mixer on to medium and add the dissolved yeast. Two minutes later, add the salt, mix for 2 minutes and then add the olive oil. Keep mixing until the dough is shiny and homogenous, about 6 minutes. Turn the speed up a little and mix for 2 minutes more.

A good way to check the elasticity is right is to stretch a piece of dough and if it forms a strong, transparent membrane without breaking (similar to blowing a bubble with gum), it is ready. Let the dough sit, covered with plastic wrap, for 30 minutes in winter or 15 minutes in summer. The dough is now ready to be shaped into balls and then rested further in the refrigerator before shaping into discs (see pages 22–25).

Makes 6 pizze (250 g/9 oz each)

Dried yeast dough

This pizza dough is made using easily available dried (powdered) yeast, which gives very consistent results. Each 250 g (9 oz) ball of dough will make one 30 cm (12 inch) pizza.

1 kg (2 lb 4 oz/6⅔ cups) unbleached, stoneground whole-wheat flour or strong bread flour
550 ml (19 fl oz) water at room temperature
2 g (1/16 oz) dried (powdered) yeast
20 g (¾ oz) sea salt
30 ml (1 fl oz) extra virgin olive oil

Place the flour and 500 ml (17 fl oz/2 cups) of the water in a mixer fitted with a dough hook attachment. Begin mixing on a low speed and keep mixing until the flour has absorbed all the water but is still not smooth. This should take only 3–4 minutes. Stop the mixer and let the dough rest in the bowl for 15–20 minutes.

Meanwhile, dissolve the yeast in the remaining water. Once the dough has rested, turn the mixer on to medium and add the dissolved yeast. Two minutes later, add the salt, mix for 2 minutes and then add the olive oil. Keep mixing until the dough is shiny and homogenous, about 6 minutes. Turn the speed up a little and mix for 2 minutes more.

A good way to check the elasticity is right is to stretch a piece of dough and if it forms a strong, transparent membrane without breaking (similar to blowing a bubble with gum), it is ready. Let the dough sit, covered with plastic wrap, for 30 minutes in winter or 15 minutes in summer. The dough is now ready to be shaped into balls and then rested further in the refrigerator before shaping into discs (see pages 22–25).

Makes 6 pizze (250 g/9 oz each)

Basic pizza dough / Indirect method

The indirect method uses two (or more) phases for producing the dough. More time and labour are involved, but the results are great in terms of flavour, texture and digestibility. Ambient, or room, temperature affects the living dough. If it is cold, the dough takes time to develop and if it's warm, it moves quickly. Resting dough outside the refrigerator requires judgment, experience and practice. In this recipe the first dough must be kept at 16–20°C (60–68°F), which may be tricky during warmer parts of the year. At Pizzaperta, we have a purpose-built cabinet that sits at around 16°C (60°F). If you have a wine cabinet, they are also excellent. Otherwise, a cellar or insulated room in the house can be used. I've even successfully improvised a portable cool box with a couple of large ice cooler bricks.

Temperature

The temperature of the final dough produced by the indirect method is important. It should be less than 24°C (75°F).

Temperature is key in controlling the activity of yeast and influencing dough structure. It prevents the formation of large air bubbles and promotes the elasticity of the dough. It can be achieved by controlling the temperature (T) of the water added to the final dough by using a simple formula:

$T_{water} = 3T_{dough} - (T_{ambient} + T_{flour} + T_{machine\ bowl})$

So, to find out the correct water temperature (T_{water}), multiply the dough temperature by 3 ($3T_{dough}$). Now add together the temperature of the room, of the flour and of the mixer machine bowl ($T_{ambient} + T_{flour} + T_{machine\ bowl}$). Take this number away from the $3T_{dough}$ and you'll have the temperature of the water to be added.

To measure these temperatures we use a combination of a normal thermometer, a probe thermometer (for the dough and flour) and an infrared gun thermometer. This last one is used for the machine bowl, though if the mixer is kept in the kitchen it's probably ambient temperature.

As an example, if the dough temperature required is 22°C, ambient 24°C, flour 18°C and machine bowl 20°C, the formula would look like this:

$T_{water} = 3 \times 22°C - (24°C + 18°C + 20°C)$ or
$T_{water} = 66°C - 62°C$

Therefore the water temperature needs to be 4°C when added. This will be the temperature of water kept in a refrigerator. If lower temperatures are required, then ice added to a little refrigerated water is fine.

For the first dough (biga)

1 kg (2 lb 4 oz/6⅔ cups) unbleached, stoneground
  whole-wheat flour or strong bread flour
450 ml (16 fl oz) water at room temperature
6 g (⅛ oz) dried (powdered) yeast

Place the flour and 400 ml (14 fl oz) of water in a mixer with a dough hook attachment. Dissolve the yeast in the remaining water.

Turn on the mixer at its lowest speed and add the dissolved yeast. Keep working until a rough dough is produced. It may take 5–6 minutes. It doesn't need to be smooth; it just needs to hold together in a rough mass.

Place the dough in a clean plastic bucket, glass or ceramic container, cover with plastic wrap or a lid and keep at a temperature between 16–20°C (60–68°F) for 16–18 hours.

For the final dough

300 g (10½ oz) biga (the first dough)
1 kg (2 lb 4 oz/6⅔ cups) unbleached, stoneground
  whole-wheat flour or strong bread flour
550 ml (19 fl oz) water at correct temperature
  (see temperature note opposite)
35 g (1¼ oz) sea salt
35 ml (1¼ fl oz) extra virgin olive oil

Place all the ingredients except the olive oil in a mixer fitted with a dough hook attachment. Work at the lowest speed for 8 minutes. When the dough is homogenous, increase the speed slightly and work for about 20 minutes or so until the gluten has developed to the point where the dough can be stretched like bubble gum.

Finally, add the olive oil and mix for 1 minute. Turn the dough onto a work surface, cover with plastic wrap and leave at ambient temperature for 30 minutes in winter or 15 minutes in summer. The dough is now ready to be shaped into balls and then rested further in the refrigerator before shaping into discs (see pages 22–25).

Makes 6 pizze (250 g/9 oz each)

Shaping basic dough into balls

Once the dough is ready to be shaped, take a bench scraper and cut off a piece from the edge.

The dough will feel soft, airy and malleable. Take the piece of dough at one end and, using both hands, form a ball about 200–250 g (7–9 oz) in size. Work by tucking the folds under the ball so that the top surface is taut and smooth.

Pinch the dough underneath the formed ball to separate it from the long piece of dough.

Repeat this procedure to make more balls.

5

Roll each ball gently on the work surface to make it even and round.

6

Place the balls on a covered non-stick tray. Make sure there is at least one ball width between each ball and the edges of the tray and that the balls don't touch the cover. Use a fine mist water spray to hydrate the surface of the balls once they are on the tray. Let rise for 1 hour at 20–24°C (68–75°F). After resting, place in a refrigerator for at least 12 hours and up to 18 hours. The balls can sit in the refrigerator at around 4–5°C (39–41°F) for up to 3 days.

Shaping basic dough into bases

Once the dough has tripled in size, remove from the fridge and leave at room temperature for 3–4 hours (less in summer and more in winter). Choose your dough ball and sprinkle flour on top and where it touches the surrounding balls.

Use the bench scraper to separate the dough ball from its neighbours.

Lift the dough ball from the tray and turn bottom side up, revealing the bubbles.

Place the dough ball, still bottom side up, on a small mound of flour and turn it over in the flour to cover both sides.

Begin by using your fingers to form the cornice (border) and push out the dough, making the circle larger.

Once the dough has doubled in circumference, remove from the flour and place on the work surface.

Keeping one hand on one side of the base, gently stretch the opposite side with the other hand and lift and slap the dough circle from side to side. This will stretch the gluten in the dough and the base will get larger and larger.

Once stretched to the desired size (our pizze are around 30 cm/12 inches in diameter), place the base back on the work surface and neaten into a circle. The pizza base is now ready to dress with the toppings and then bake.

Roman-style pizza dough / Basic

Roman-style pizza is a rectangular, focaccia-like pizza that is famous in Rome. It is light, full of large bubbles and can be filled or topped with many ingredients. Roman-style pizza does not require a wood-fired oven, but traditionally is cooked in a 'deck' oven at almost half the temperature of wood-fired pizza. Use stoneground whole-wheat (not wholemeal) flour.

1 kg (2 lb 4 oz/6⅔ cups)
 unbleached, stoneground whole-
 wheat flour or strong bread flour
3.5 g (⅛ oz) dried (powdered) yeast
650 ml (23 fl oz) water at room
 temperature
½ teaspoon caster (superfine) sugar
25 ml (1 fl oz) extra virgin olive oil
20 g (¾ oz) sea salt

Place the flour in a mixer with a dough hook attachment.

Dissolve the yeast in 100 ml (3½ fl oz) of the water and add to the flour along with 400 ml (14 fl oz) of the remaining water and the caster sugar.

Turn on the mixer to its lowest setting and mix for about 2 minutes until the water is totally absorbed. Add the oil and salt and mix in. Double the speed of the mixer and slowly add the remaining water, a little at a time, only adding more when the previous amount has been absorbed. The mixture will look quite wet, but don't worry, continue mixing for 8–10 minutes and you'll see that gradually the dough will begin to stretch and form long gluten strands.

Rest the dough for 10 minutes in the mixer bowl, covered with plastic wrap, before folding, leaving to mature in the refrigerator and forming into three sheets (teglie) of Roman-style pizza dough (see pages 28–30).

Makes 3 teglie (550 g/1 lb 4 oz sheets)

Roman-style pizza dough / Mixed wheat

This recipe produces a full-flavoured, fragrant Roman-style pizza dough and can be substituted for the basic Roman-style pizza dough quite successfully in any recipe. The method is based on a recipe from Rome's Gabriele Bonci. Once again, the flours used are the most important factor. The best results are obtained by using stoneground, whole-wheat types. I use Italian flours such as Petra or Mulino Marino, but any good whole-wheat flour will work well.

500 g (1 lb 2 oz/3⅓ cups) unbleached, stoneground whole-wheat flour or strong bread flour
200 g (7 oz/1⅓ cups) wholemeal flour
200 g (7 oz/2 cups) stoneground 'white' spelt flour
100 g (3½ oz/¾ cup) rye flour
3 g (⅛ oz) dried (powdered) yeast
800 ml (28 fl oz) water at room temperature
25 ml (1 fl oz) extra virgin olive oil
15 g (½ oz) sea salt

Mix all the flours together in a mixer with a beater attachment.

In a small bowl, dissolve the yeast in 50 ml (1¾ fl oz) of the water. Add this, along with 550 ml (19 fl oz) of the water, the oil and salt to the flour and mix on the lowest speed. Once the dough comes together, change the beater attachment to the dough attachment, double the mixer speed and continue mixing, adding the rest of the water, a little at a time, until it's all absorbed. The mixture will look quite wet, but don't worry: continue mixing for 8–10 minutes and gradually the dough will begin to stretch and form long gluten strands.

Rest the dough for 10 minutes in the mixer bowl, covered with plastic wrap, before folding, leaving to mature in the refrigerator and forming into three sheets (teglie) of Roman-style pizza dough (see pages 28–30).

Makes 3 teglie (550 g/1 lb 4 oz sheets)

Shaping Roman-style dough

FOLDING / Once the dough has rested, it needs to be folded to give it strength. Lightly oil your hands and work surface with extra virgin olive oil. Tip the dough out onto the work surface. Lift it gently in the centre and fold the ends under (or over) to meet in the middle to form pockets of air.

Turn the dough 90 degrees and repeat the fold. Return to the bowl, cover with plastic wrap and rest for 15 minutes, then fold again. Rest for another 15 minutes, then do a final fold as before. Place the dough in an oiled, plastic container with an airtight lid and leave for 18–24 hours in the refrigerator.

Once the dough has matured in the refrigerator, turn out from the container on to the work surface. Divide the dough into three pieces.

Shape each piece of dough. Place your hands under the outer edges and slide under to form a ball. Repeat several times until the dough has a ball-like appearance.

5

Fold and gather with your fingers at the edge of each piece of dough, bringing the ball towards you – this will make it even and smooth. Leave the dough balls at room temperature in three oiled containers for 2 hours to rise.

6

STRETCHING / Oil an oven tray (teglia) or baking tray with extra virgin olive oil.

7

Sprinkle the work surface lightly with flour and turn out one piece of the dough.

8

Begin to press gently on the surface of the dough with your fingers, stretching it to roughly fit the size of the tray.

Transfer the dough to the baking tray, gently supporting the dough with as much of your arms as possible.

Stretch the dough gently to fit and then make delicate indents on the surface with your fingers.

Sprinkle some extra virgin olive oil on the surface and then gently spread it with your fingers. The pizza is now ready to be dressed with toppings or to go directly into the oven to be precooked.

Cooking basic dough

Shaped and topped, here you'll find instructions for cooking your round pizze.

In a wood-fired oven

With the floor temperature between 360–400°C (680–750°F), a pizza will take around 90 seconds to cook. Some pizzaioli cook at temperatures up to 450°C (840°F) and this takes less time. The pizza is put directly on to the oven floor to cook, thereby getting an immediate 'lift'.

In a domestic oven

My suggestion is to find a large terracotta tile that fits onto your oven rack. Place the rack on the bottom rung of your oven and the tile on top, giving you plenty of room above to manipulate the pizza. Turn to full heat without using any fan-forced function and let the oven run for at least 20 minutes to heat the tile completely. When the pizza is ready, use a floured paddle to take it from the bench on to the tile. Close the oven immediately.

At around 250–280°C (480–535°F) a pizza takes 3–5 minutes to cook, depending on your oven temperature. It will have a crisp, bread-like texture and should be no less delicious than the wood-fired version.

Cooking Roman-style dough

Roman-style pizza is often precooked. It's convenient because the cooked dough can be kept in the fridge and brought out, topped and heated in the oven when needed.

Preheat the oven to 250°C (500°F) without fan.

Take the sheet of Roman-style pizza dough and if the dough has risen excessively, press down gently with the tips of your fingers to make small indentations.

Bake the pizza in the oven for 11–14 minutes. If the teglia is browning more on one side, your oven is not even and the tray may need to be turned.

Once cooked, remove from the oven and let cool a little before dressing with your toppings or allow to cool completely if using later. The teglia can be wrapped tightly with plastic wrap and stored in the refrigerator for up to 3 days.

OPPOSITE / San Marzano tomatoes are grown in the volcanic soil of the foothills beneath Mount Vesuvius. These wooden stakes attest to the laborious manual work carried out each year by the farmers. **THIS PAGE** / The San Marzano tomato harvest.

Margherita

Along with the Marinara, the Margherita represents the classic pizza of Naples. In fact, there are still places that only serve these two pizze. The Margherita is perhaps the world's most iconic pizza.

250 g (9 oz) ball of basic pizza dough (see pages 18–21), shaped (see pages 22–25)

80–100 g (3–3½ oz/⅓ cup) tinned San Marzano whole peeled tomatoes

150 g (5½ oz) fior di latte mozzarella
A handful of fresh basil leaves
1 tablespoon extra virgin olive oil

TO ASSEMBLE / Place a large tile in your oven for the pizza, then preheat to full heat (without using any fan-forced function) for at least 20 minutes (see page 31). Hand squeeze the tomatoes; it doesn't matter if there are pieces left and they're not completely uniform. Spread onto the shaped pizza base, leaving the edges clear to about 3–4 cm (1½ inches). Thinly slice the mozzarella and scatter evenly, here and there, on the tomato. Place the basil leaves on top. Place the pizza in the oven for 3–5 minutes until cooked, turning to get an even colour. Remove and drizzle with the oil.

Makes one 30 cm (12 inch) pizza

Roman margherita

Although on a Roman-style base, this tomato-topped pizza has the same ingredients as a classic Naples Margherita. The main difference is that the mozzarella is torn in pieces and scattered on the surface after it's taken from the oven.

1 sheet of Roman-style pizza dough
  (see pages 26–30)

350 g (12 oz/1⅓ cups) tinned San
  Marzano whole peeled tomatoes
2 tablespoons extra virgin olive oil
Pinch of sea salt
400 g (14 oz) fior di latte mozzarella
100 g (3½ oz/2 cups) fresh basil
  leaves

TO ASSEMBLE / Preheat the oven to 220°C (425°F). Hand squeeze the tomatoes until they're uniformly mashed and mix in a tablespoon of extra virgin olive oil and a pinch of salt. Spread the tomato mixture on top of the sheet of pizza as evenly as possible. If the dough has risen excessively, press down gently with the tips of your fingers to make small indentations to trap the tomato. Bake in the oven for 25 minutes. If the teglia is browning more on one side, your oven is not even and the tray may need to be turned. Once cooked, remove from the oven and let cool a little. Place on a serving plate as a large piece or cut, using scissors, into individual tiles. Remove the mozzarella from the water. Tear into small pieces and distribute on top of the pizza. Scatter the basil leaves on top and finish with the remaining extra virgin olive oil.

Serves 6–8

Roman pizza with figs, prosciutto and balsamic

There is way too much balsamic vinegar used these days. And most of it is that poor supermarket-bought tangy brown liquid sweetened with caramel. If you're going to use balsamic in this classic combination, spend a little more on the good stuff. It's well worth it.

1 sheet of Roman-style pizza dough
(see pages 26–30), precooked
(see page 31) and cut into
8 squares

8 ripe figs, sliced into 5 mm (¼ inch)
rounds
16 thin slices of Prosciutto di Parma
or similar
2 teaspoons aged balsamic vinegar
Sea salt and freshly ground black
pepper

TO ASSEMBLE / Cut each pizza square in half, opening it to form a 'sandwich'. Place the halves back together on a baking tray and heat in a preheated 180°C (350°F) oven for 5–6 minutes until they are crisp on the outside but soft in the middle. Once ready, remove from the oven. Place the bottoms of each square on the work surface and lay the slices of fig down first. Next, add two slices of prosciutto per square. Finally, sprinkle with the balsamic, season lightly with salt and freshly ground pepper and place the top half of the square on each.

Makes 8 filled Roman pizze

Marinara Napoletana

*This is the classic, and perhaps original, Neapolitan pizza. There are few ingredients –
no cheese and no seafood!*

250 g (9 oz) ball of basic pizza
   dough (see pages 18–21), shaped
   (see pages 22–25)

100 g (3½ oz/⅓ cup) tinned
   San Marzano whole peeled
   tomatoes
A pinch of sea salt
1 garlic clove, crushed
2 tablespoons extra virgin olive oil
2–3 good pinches of best-quality
   dried oregano
1 garlic clove, thinly sliced

TO ASSEMBLE / Place a large tile in your oven for the pizza, then preheat to
full heat (without using any fan-forced function) for at least 20 minutes (see page
31). Squeeze the tomatoes by hand or with a fork until they're uniformly mashed
and mix in a pinch of salt. Mix the crushed garlic and olive oil together. Spread
the mashed tomato onto the shaped pizza base, leaving the edges clear to
about 3–4 cm (1½ inches). Scatter the dried oregano over the tomato. Drizzle
half the oil and garlic mixture over the tomato. Distribute the garlic slices here and
there. Place the pizza in the oven for 3–5 minutes until cooked, turning to get an
even colour. Remove and drizzle with the remaining oil.

Makes one 30 cm (12 inch) pizza

Quattro formaggi and walnuts

*Here's another take on a modern classic – the four cheeses. You could make it five by adding
a final sprinkling of grated Parmigiano. I've added walnuts and quite a bit of pepper.*

250 g (9 oz) ball of basic pizza
   dough (see pages 18–21), shaped
   (see pages 22–25)

120 g (4¼ oz) fior di latte mozzarella
80 g (3 oz/⅓ cup) ricotta cheese
80 g (3 oz) gorgonzola cheese, cut
   into 1 cm (½ inch) cubes
100 g (3½ oz/1 cup) grated pecorino
   cheese
120 g (4¼ oz/1 cup) fresh, shelled
   walnut pieces
½ teaspoon freshly ground black
   pepper

TO ASSEMBLE / Place a large tile in your oven for the pizza, then turn the
oven up to preheat to full heat (without using any fan-forced function) for at least
20 minutes (see page 31). Thinly slice the mozzarella and scatter evenly, here
and there, to top the shaped pizza base, leaving the edges clear to about
3–4 cm (1½ inches). Spoon the ricotta in blobs over the mozzarella and place
the gorgonzola cubes randomly in places where there is no ricotta. Scatter
pecorino evenly over the lot and distribute the walnut pieces throughout. Finally,
season with the black pepper and place the pizza in the oven for 3–5 minutes
until cooked, turning to get an even colour.

Makes one 30 cm (12 inch) pizza

OPPOSITE / These centuries-old Puglian trees still produce olives. **THIS PAGE** / Structures called trulli are a feature of the landscape of central Puglia.

Roman pizza with red onion

This is more of a snack pizza, which can be cut into fingers and eaten with antipasto or served as a base for topping with things like caponata, chopped roast vegetables, salami or even cooked sausage.

1 sheet of Roman-style pizza dough (see pages 26–30)

2 tablespoons extra virgin olive oil
1 kg (2 lb 4 oz) red onions, thinly sliced
Sea salt and freshly ground black pepper

TO ASSEMBLE / Heat the olive oil in a heavy-based frying pan and gently fry the onion for 2 minutes. Remove from the heat, season to taste and let the onion cool. Preheat the oven to 220°C (425°F). Spread the onion on top of the sheet of pizza as evenly as possible. If the dough has risen excessively, press down gently with the tips of your fingers to make small indentations. If there is any oil in the pan from cooking the onion, scatter it on top of the dough. Bake in the oven for 25 minutes. If the teglia is browning more on one side, your oven is not even and the tray may need to be turned. Once cooked, remove from the oven and the pizza is ready to use. It can be cut into pieces and used as bread or topped with anything appropriate. It can also be wrapped and stored in the refrigerator for up to 4 days and is excellent reheated.

Serves 6–8

Chargrilled vegetables

The vegetables on this pizza can (and should) change with the seasons. Leeks would work well in winter or thin slices of squash or pumpkin. Similarly, asparagus in spring and string beans in summer go nicely, as would any vegetable that can be chargrilled.

250 g (9 oz) ball of basic pizza
    dough (see pages 18–21), shaped
    (see pages 22–23)

1 red onion, skin left on, halved
80 g (3 oz/⅓ cup) tinned San
    Marzano whole peeled tomatoes
150 g (5½ oz) fior di latte mozzarella
50 g (2 oz/½ cup) grated parmesan
    cheese

CHARGRILLED VEGETABLES
1 zucchini (courgette), trimmed and cut
    lengthways into 3 mm (⅛ inch) slices
½ eggplant (aubergine), trimmed and
    cut into 3 mm (⅛ inch) slices
Sea salt and freshly ground black
    pepper
Extra virgin olive oil

TO ASSEMBLE / Season all the vegetable slices except the onion, add a little extra virgin olive oil and chargrill for about 30 seconds on each side until tender. Brush the onion with olive oil and place in a 200°C (400°F) oven for about 15–20 minutes or until tender all the way to the centre. Remove the outer skin and tough leaves of flesh and separate out the tender flesh to use on the pizza.

Place a large tile in your oven for the pizza, then turn the oven up to preheat to full heat (without using any fan-forced function) for at least 20 minutes (see page 31). Hand squeeze the tomatoes; it doesn't matter if there are pieces left and they're not completely uniform. Spread onto the shaped pizza base, leaving the edges clear to about 3–4 cm (1½ inches). Thinly slice the mozzarella and scatter evenly, here and there, on the tomato. Scatter the grated parmesan and then the vegetables evenly over the surface, making sure not to pile too much on. Place in the oven for 3–5 minutes until cooked, turning to get an even colour. Remove and drizzle with 1 tablespoon of the extra virgin olive oil.

Makes one 30 cm (12 inch) pizza

Roman pizza with gorgonzola and figs

If you've ever had a dry red wine with gorgonzola, or other sharp blue cheeses, you'll know that it's not a great match. A reaction occurs whereby a metallic-like taste is left in your mouth. Sweet things are far more complementary, like sweet wine and, in this case, figs. Choose figs that are at the peak of their ripeness and sweetness.

1 sheet of Roman-style pizza dough
(see pages 26–30)

20 ripe green or black figs
2 tablespoons extra virgin olive oil
200 g (7 oz) gorgonzola piccante
  cheese

TO ASSEMBLE / Preheat the oven to 220°C (425°F). Peel half the figs and cut each into six top to bottom. Cut the rest the same way, but leave them unpeeled. Take the sheet of pizza, scatter the peeled figs evenly over the sheet and sprinkle over the extra virgin olive oil. If the dough has risen excessively, press down gently with the tips of your fingers to make the surface flat to hold the figs. Bake in the oven for 25 minutes. If the teglia is browning more on one side, your oven is not even and the tray may need to be turned. The figs should be soft and partly caramelised. Once cooked, remove from the oven and let cool a little. Place on a serving plate as a large piece or cut, using scissors, into individual tiles. Distribute the remaining unpeeled fig segments on top. Cut the gorgonzola into small pieces and distribute on top of the pizza.

Serves 6–8

RIGHT / Streets of Altamura in Puglia.

Sicilian capers and anchovies

This is the pizza for the anchovy lover. It combines all those salty, sea-breezy flavours of the Mediterranean. Remember to use the best ingredients, especially the capers. They should be salted, not pickled.

250 g (9 oz) ball of basic pizza dough (see pages 18–21), shaped (see pages 22–25)

80 g (3 oz/⅓ cup) tinned San Marzano whole peeled tomatoes

100 g (3½ oz) fior di latte mozzarella

2 tablespoons Sicilian capers, soaked to desalt

6 large or 12 small anchovies

12 Gaeta (or similar) black olives, pitted

2–3 pinches of best-quality dried oregano

A pinch of sea salt

1 tablespoon extra virgin olive oil

TO ASSEMBLE / Place a large tile in your oven for the pizza, then preheat to full heat (without using any fan-forced function) for at least 20 minutes (see page 31). Hand squeeze the tomatoes. It doesn't matter if there are pieces left and they're not completely uniform. Spread onto the shaped pizza base, leaving the edges clear to about 3–4 cm (1½ inches). Thinly slice the mozzarella and scatter evenly, here and there, on the tomato. Scatter with the desalted capers and place the anchovies evenly over the pizza. Do the same with the olives and oregano. Season with a little salt and cook the pizza in the oven for 3–5 minutes until cooked, turning to get an even colour. Once out of the oven, drizzle with the olive oil.

Makes one 30 cm (12 inch) pizza

Black truffle and fontina

We make this pizza during the winter black truffle season. The only thing that's better to use is fresh white truffle. Use a purpose-made truffle shaver to thinly slice the truffle and cover the pizza. Fontina is a cow's milk washed-rind cheese from the northwestern Italian alpine region of Valle d'Aosta.

250 g (9 oz) ball of basic pizza dough (see pages 18–21), shaped (see pages 22–25)

120 g (4¼ oz) fontina cheese
50 g (2 oz/½ cup) grated parmesan cheese
Sea salt and freshly ground black pepper
5–10 g (⅛–¼ oz) fresh black truffle

TO ASSEMBLE / Place a large tile in your oven for the pizza, then turn the oven up to preheat to full heat (without using any fan-forced function) for at least 20 minutes (see page 31). Thinly slice the fontina and scatter evenly, here and there, to top the shaped pizza base, leaving the edges clear to about 3–4 cm (1½ inches). Sprinkle the parmesan evenly over the lot. Finally, season with a couple of pinches of salt and freshly ground pepper and place the pizza into the oven for 3–5 minutes until cooked, turning to get an even colour. Once out of the oven, shave the black truffle immediately on the pizza as the heat will release the truffle's aroma. Serve straightaway.

Makes one 30 cm (12 inch) pizza

OPPOSITE / Gabriele Bonci's pizza creations at Pizzarium in Rome are Italian street food of the highest quality.
THIS PAGE / Ordering at the counter at Pizzarium.

Classic calzone

Literally translated, a calzone is a big sock. It's the classic Neapolitan filled pizza. Once you've mastered the method of folding and cooking, you can fill it with your own ingredients. Remember not to fill it too much.

250 g (9 oz) ball of basic pizza dough (see pages 18–21), shaped as you would a normal round pizza (see pages 22–25)

100 g (3½ oz/½ cup) ricotta cheese

100 g (3½ oz) salame napoletano, sliced and then cut into strips

80 g (3 oz) fior di latte mozzarella, cut into 1 cm (½ inch) cubes, plus 6 thin slices

3–4 good pinches of freshly ground black pepper

1 tablespoon extra virgin olive oil

4 tablespoons tinned San Marzano whole peeled tomatoes, puréed

TO ASSEMBLE / Place a large tile in your oven for the pizza, then preheat to full heat (without using any fan-forced function) for at least 20 minutes (see page 31). Spread the ricotta gently on half of the dough surface, keeping about 2 cm (¾ inch) from the edges. Scatter salame strips on top and then the cubes of mozzarella. I don't add salt because the salame is salty already. Instead, add the pepper and finally drizzle over the olive oil. Fold the dough over, making a half-moon shape. Press the edges together to seal. Now make a 3 cm (1¼ inch) diameter hole in the dough on the very top, in the middle of the calzone. This will allow steam to escape while the calzone is cooking.

Spoon the tomato in a thin layer over the top of the calzone and place the mozzarella slices along. Place the pizza in the oven for 3–5 minutes until cooked, turning to get an even colour. Remove once cooked.

Makes one 30 cm (12 inch) long calzone

Pickled lettuce, capers, olives and tomatoes

This is an unusual topping for pizza. If good-quality vinegar is used when pickling the lettuce and the leaves are squeezed to expel all the liquid before using on the pizza, then the result is excellent.

250 g (9 oz) ball of basic pizza dough (see pages 18–21), shaped (see pages 22–25)

100 g (3½ oz) fior di latte mozzarella
40 g (1½ oz/¾ cup) grated parmesan
12 Gaeta (or similar) black olives
2 tablespoons Sicilian capers

CONFIT TOMATOES

1 kg (2 lb 4 oz) ripe date, cherry or any small tomatoes
6 garlic cloves, halved
3–4 sprigs of fresh thyme
Sea salt and freshly ground black pepper
150 ml (5 fl oz) extra virgin olive oil

PICKLED LETTUCE

500 g (1 lb 2 oz) lettuce leaves, various types
3 garlic cloves, halved
1 tablespoon red or white wine vinegar
2 tablespoons extra virgin olive oil

FOR THE CONFIT TOMATOES / Preheat the oven to 140°C (275°F). Cut the tomatoes in half, top to bottom. Place in an oven dish so that the tomatoes fill the bottom of the dish in one layer. Add the garlic and thyme. Season with three to four good pinches of salt and three to four turns of freshly ground pepper. Add the olive oil and mix everything carefully with a spoon. Place in the oven for 30–40 minutes. The tomatoes are ready when they're soft but not falling apart. Any extra tomatoes can be cooled and stored in the refrigerator, in a covered container, with all their cooking juices, for up to 10 days.

FOR THE PICKLED LETTUCE / Place in a large sink and wash well to remove any sand or grit. Bring a large pot of water to the boil. Add the lettuce and blanch for 2 minutes. Drain well and place the leaves in a large bowl with the garlic cloves, vinegar and extra virgin olive oil. Season to taste with salt and pepper and toss well. Make sure the lettuce is squeezed well, expelling as much liquid as possible. Any left-over lettuce will keep for up to 3 days.

TO ASSEMBLE / Place a large tile in your oven for the pizza, then turn the oven up to preheat to full heat (without using any fan-forced function) for at least 20 minutes (see page 31). Thinly slice the mozzarella and scatter evenly, here and there, to top the shaped pizza base, leaving the edges clear to 3–4 cm (1½ inches). Sprinkle with the parmesan. Evenly distribute six to eight leaves of the pickled lettuce, the olives, capers and eighteen well-drained confit tomato halves on top. Place the pizza in the oven for 3–5 minutes until cooked, turning to get an even colour. Once cooked, finish with pepper and serve immediately.

Makes one 30 cm (12 inch) pizza

Roman pizza with eggplant parmigiana

Everybody loves a good eggplant parmigiana. This is a homage to that great dish, albeit in the shape of a Roman pizza.

1 sheet of Roman-style pizza dough
(see pages 26–30), precooked
(see page 31) and cut into
8 squares

8 slices of fior di latte mozzarella
16 slices of smoked scamorza cheese
24 slices of chargrilled eggplant
(aubergine) (see page 48)
8 tablespoons grated parmesan cheese
2 tablespoons shaved parmesan
cheese
24 confit tomatoes (see page 60)
8 sprigs of fresh basil

SAN MARZANO SAUCE
4 tablespoons extra virgin olive oil
1 onion, minced
2 garlic cloves, crushed
650 g (1 lb 7 oz/2½ cups) tinned
San Marzano whole peeled
tomatoes, puréed
25 g (1 oz/½ cup) fresh basil leaves,
roughly torn
Sea salt and freshly ground black
pepper

FOR THE SAN MARZANO SAUCE / Heat the olive oil in a pan and gently fry the onion and garlic until transparent. Add the tomato and basil. Season with a couple of pinches of salt and a little pepper. Stir well and simmer slowly until the sauce thickens and most of the water has evaporated. Depending on the tomatoes, this should take 10–15 minutes. Any extra tomato sauce can be stored in the refrigerator for 5–6 days.

TO ASSEMBLE / Cut each pizza square in half, opening it to form a 'sandwich'. Place the halves on a baking tray. On the bottom half of each place one slice of mozzarella and two slices of scamorza. Heat in a preheated 180°C (350°F) oven for 4–5 minutes until they are crisp on the outside but soft in the middle and the cheese has melted. Once ready, remove from the oven and on each bottom half place three pieces of chargrilled eggplant, 2 tablespoons San Marzano sauce and a tablespoon of grated parmesan. Close each with the top half of the pizza square and finish with some shaved parmesan, three confit tomatoes and a sprig of basil.

Makes 8 filled Roman pizze

Roman pizza with tomato and stracciatella

This is such a simple pizza, dressed with few ingredients. The stracciatella makes the preparation luxuriously rich and creamy. Stracciatella is a mixture of fine mozzarella strands mixed with cream. It can be used by itself and is featured as the filling in the extraordinary burrata cheese, originating in Puglia.

1 sheet of Roman-style pizza dough
 (see pages 26–30)

300 g (10½ oz/1¼ cups) tinned
 San Marzano peeled tomatoes
2 tablespoons extra virgin olive oil
Sea salt and freshly ground black
 pepper
350 g (12 oz) stracciatella cheese
50 g (2 oz/1 cup) fresh basil leaves

TO ASSEMBLE / Preheat the oven to 220°C (425°F). Hand squeeze the tomatoes until they're uniformly mashed and mix in a tablespoon of extra virgin olive oil and a pinch of salt. Spread the tomato mixture on top of the sheet of pizza as evenly as possible. If the dough has risen excessively, press down gently with the tips of your fingers to make small indentations to trap the tomato. Bake in the oven for 25 minutes. If the teglia is browning more on one side, your oven is not even and the tray may need to be turned. Once cooked, remove from the oven and let cool a little. Place on a serving plate as a large piece or cut into individual tiles. Using your fingers, distribute the stracciatella, here and there, on top of the pizza. Scatter basil leaves on top and finish with the remaining extra virgin olive oil and some freshly ground pepper.

Serves 6–8

Pancetta, wilted rucola and taleggio

Taleggio is a washed-rind, soft cheese with a strong flavour from Italy's Lombardy region. It tones down somewhat on cooking, but the smellier, the better. I love using rocket as a cooked ingredient rather than just as a salad leaf. Here it adds colour as well as a spicy note.

250 g (9 oz) ball of basic pizza
   dough (see pages 18–21), shaped
   (see pages 22–25)

100 g (3½ oz/3 cups) rocket
   (arugula), thick stems removed
100 g (3½ oz) fior di latte mozzarella
1 tablespoon grated parmesan cheese
100 g (3½ oz) taleggio cheese, cut
   into small cubes
A couple of pinches of freshly ground
   black pepper
12 slices of good-quality pancetta
1 tablespoon extra virgin olive oil

TO ASSEMBLE / Place a large tile in your oven for the pizza, then preheat to full heat (without using any fan-forced function) for at least 20 minutes (see page 31). Bring a pot of salted water to the boil. Plunge in the rocket leaves, submerging them using a wooden spoon. Blanch for 2 minutes, drain and let cool before squeezing well to expel most of the water and roughly chopping.

Thinly slice the mozzarella and scatter evenly, here and there, to top the shaped pizza base, leaving the edges clear to about 3–4 cm (1½ inches). Arrange the cooked, chopped rocket on the mozzarella and sprinkle the parmesan over the lot. Place the pizza in the oven for 3–5 minutes until cooked, turning to get an even colour. Once out of the oven, arrange the taleggio on top, sprinkle with pepper, drape the pancetta over and drizzle with the olive oil.

Makes one 30 cm (12 inch) pizza

Roman pizza with prosciutto, burrata and eggplant

I first had this combination at Antonio Pappalardo's Cascina dei Sapori in Rezzato, Brescia. I fell in love with the richness of the burrata and the salty goodness of the prosciutto. Above all, I loved the base – soft and airy inside and crisp on the outside

1 sheet of Roman-style pizza dough (see pages 26–30), precooked (see page 31) and cut into 8 squares

8 thin slices of hot chargrilled eggplant (aubergine) (see page 48)
8 thin slices of Prosciutto di Parma or similar
1 or 2 burrata, depending on size, cut into 8 in a bowl
Sea salt and freshly ground black pepper

TO ASSEMBLE / Place the Roman pizza squares on a baking tray and heat in a preheated 180°C (350°F) oven for 5–6 minutes until they are crisp on the outside but soft in the middle. Once ready, remove from the oven. Form a cup using a piece of hot chargrilled eggplant in the middle and a slice of prosciutto on the outside. Place this neatly on each square and arrange on plates. Spoon the burrata into the middle of the cup. The burrata will fall apart because it is soft, but can be handled using a tablespoon. Season lightly with salt and freshly ground pepper.

Makes 8 squares

NEXT PAGE / Looking south along the Naples coastline.

Tuna, Mediterranean herbs and colatura

Colatura is the ancient fish sauce the Romans once used and it is still being made from salted anchovies in Cetara on the Amalfi Coast, south of Naples.

250 g (9 oz) ball of basic pizza dough (see pages 18–21), shaped (see pages 22–25)

1 tablespoon extra virgin olive oil
1 teaspoon colatura d'alici
1 small garlic clove, crushed
1 tablespoon fresh basil, finely chopped
1 tablespoon fresh parsley, finely chopped
½ teaspoon best-quality dried oregano
160 g (5½ oz) piece of tuna, cut into 1 cm (½ inch) cubes
80 g (3 oz/⅓ cup) tinned San Marzano whole peeled tomatoes
80 g (3 oz) fior di latte mozzarella
½ red onion, thinly sliced
10 Gaeta (or similar) black olives, pitted
1 tablespoon Sicilian capers, soaked to desalt

TO ASSEMBLE / Place a large tile in your oven for the pizza, then preheat to full heat (without using any fan-forced function) for at least 20 minutes (see page 31). Mix the olive oil, colatura and garlic together and set apart in a small bowl. Next, mix the chopped basil and parsley with the dried oregano and toss with the tuna cubes until they're well coated and set aside.

Hand squeeze the tomatoes; it doesn't matter if there are pieces left and they're not completely uniform. Spread the squeezed tomato onto the shaped pizza base, leaving the edges clear to 3–4 cm (1½ inches). Thinly slice the mozzarella and scatter evenly, here and there, on top of the tomato. Scatter the onion around and place the herbed tuna cubes on top along with the olives and capers. Place the pizza in the oven for 3–5 minutes until cooked, turning to get an even colour. Remove and drizzle with the oil, garlic and colatura mixture.

Makes one 30 cm (12 inch) pizza

Capocollo and fennel

Capocollo is pork neck, salted and dried like prosciutto. Some of the very best comes from around the city of Martina Franca in Puglia. Most good Italian butchers will make their own version.

250 g (9 oz) ball of basic pizza
    dough (see pages 18–21), shaped
    (see pages 22–25)

100 g (3½ oz) fior di latte mozzarella
70 g (2½ oz/½ cup) thinly sliced
    fennel, plus 8 fennel fronds
8 slices of capocollo di Martina
    Franca
2 tablespoons grated pecorino cheese
1 tablespoon extra virgin olive oil
A couple of pinches of freshly ground
    black pepper

TO ASSEMBLE / Place a large tile in your oven for the pizza, then turn the oven up to preheat to full heat (without using any fan-forced function) for at least 20 minutes (see page 31). Thinly slice the mozzarella and scatter evenly, here and there, to top the shaped pizza base, leaving the edges clear to about 3–4 cm (1½ inches). Scatter the fennel evenly over the pizza. Place the pizza in the oven for 3–5 minutes until cooked, turning to get an even colour. Once out of the oven, place the capocollo slices over the pizza. Sprinkle the pecorino on top and distribute the fennel fronds over the lot. Drizzle with the olive oil and add a little black pepper.

Makes one 30 cm (12 inch) pizza

Roman pizza with zucchini trifolati

Many of the toppings on these pizze are built on memories from my childhood. In discussing this particular pizza with Pizzaperta chef Gianluca, we discovered we had similar memories of zucchini (courgette) trifolati. Both our mothers prepared this dish in a similar way, though at different ends of the peninsula – Brescia and Naples. 'Trifolati' is an Italian cooking term that denotes frying in olive oil, garlic and parsley. It is most often applied to mushrooms, kidneys and zucchini.

1 sheet of Roman-style pizza dough
   (see pages 26–30)

350 g (12 oz) fior di latte mozzarella
Sea salt and freshly ground black
   pepper
1 tablespoon extra virgin olive oil

ZUCCHINI TRIFOLATI
1 small onion, thinly sliced
500 g (1 lb 2 oz) zucchini
   (courgettes), cut into thin rounds
2 garlic cloves, crushed
3 tablespoons extra virgin olive oil
2 tinned San Marzano whole peeled
   tomatoes, chopped
2 tablespoons finely chopped fresh
   flat-leaf parsley
Sea salt and freshly ground black
   pepper

FOR THE ZUCCHINI TRIFOLATI / Fry the onion, zucchini and garlic in the olive oil for 2 minutes over a high heat, keeping them stirred so they don't colour. Add the tomato and simmer for 15 minutes. Add the chopped parsley, season with salt and pepper and mix well. Leave to cool completely. Any left-over zucchini can be refrigerated for 3–4 days.

TO ASSEMBLE / Preheat the oven to 220°C (425°F). Place the cooked and cooled zucchini trifolati in a sieve to drain its liquid, saving some of the liquid. Remove the mozzarella from the water. Tear into small pieces and distribute half on top of the sheet of pizza. Scatter 400 g (14 oz) of the well-drained zucchini trifolati on the mozzarella. Distribute the rest of the torn mozzarella on the zucchini. Finally, season with a little salt and freshly ground black pepper and drizzle with the olive oil. If the dough has risen excessively, press down gently with the tips of your fingers to make small indentations to make space for the mozzarella and zucchini. Bake in the oven for 25 minutes. If the teglia is browning more on one side, your oven is not even and the tray may need to be turned. Once cooked, remove from oven and let cool a little. Place on a serving plate as a large piece or cut, using scissors, into individual tiles. Finish by drizzling with some of the zucchini trifolati juices that have been drained.

Serves 6–8

Smoked leg ham, mushroom and sage

This is a lovely combination of flavours, especially between the smoked leg ham and the sage. Don't buy pre-packaged ham, but rather have it sliced off the bone and ask for it a little thicker for texture.

250 g (9 oz) ball of basic pizza
  dough (see pages 18–21), shaped
  (see pages 26–30)

50 ml (2 fl oz/¼ cup) extra virgin
  olive oil, for frying, plus
  1 tablespoon for drizzling
12 large fresh sage leaves
80 g (3 oz/⅓ cup) tinned San
  Marzano whole peeled tomatoes
100 g (3½ oz) fior di latte mozzarella
90 g (3½ oz) smoked leg ham,
  shaved
90 g (3½ oz/1 cup) thinly sliced
  button or small cap mushrooms
Sea salt and freshly ground black
  pepper

TO ASSEMBLE / Place a large tile in your oven for the pizza, then preheat to full heat (without using any fan-forced function) for at least 20 minutes (see page 31). Heat the extra virgin olive oil in a small saucepan and fry the sage leaves until crisp. Remove from the oil and drain on some paper towel.

Hand squeeze the tomatoes; it doesn't matter if there are pieces left and they're not completely uniform. Spread the squeezed tomato onto the shaped pizza base, leaving the edges clear to about 3–4 cm (1½ inches). Thinly slice the mozzarella and scatter evenly, here and there, on the tomato. Scatter the ham and mushrooms evenly over the pizza. Season with a little salt and a couple of turns of the pepper mill and cook in the oven for 3–5 minutes until cooked, turning to get an even colour. Once out of the oven, drizzle with the remaining olive oil and scatter the fried sage on top.

Makes one 30 cm (12 inch) pizza

Calamari, chilli and ginger

This is a combination I use in various dishes and it works well on this pizza. In fact, the most recent ingredient in this combination to arrive in Europe is the chilli. Ginger was used extensively by the Romans not only as a digestive, but as a flavouring too.

250 g (9 oz) ball of basic pizza dough (see pages 18–21), shaped (see pages 22–25)

2 tablespoons extra virgin olive oil
180 g (6½ oz) cleaned calamari (squid), patted dry with paper towel
1 garlic clove, crushed
1–2 chillies, finely sliced
1 teaspoon finely chopped fresh ginger
Sea salt
1 tablespoon finely chopped fresh parsley
80 g (3 oz/⅓ cup) tinned San Marzano whole peeled tomatoes
80 g (3 oz) fior di latte mozzarella

TO ASSEMBLE / Place a large tile in your oven for the pizza, then preheat to full heat (without using any fan-forced function) for at least 20 minutes (see page 31). Heat the olive oil in a heavy-based frying pan. Once it starts to smoke, carefully add the calamari, garlic, chilli and ginger. Fry over a high heat for a minute or so until just cooked. Season with salt, mix in the parsley and set aside to cool. Once cool, drain any oil or liquid from the calamari and reserve.

Hand squeeze the tomatoes; it doesn't matter if there are pieces left and they're not completely uniform. Spread the squeezed tomato onto the shaped pizza base, leaving the edges clear to 3–4 cm (1½ inches). Thinly slice the mozzarella and scatter evenly, here and there, on top of the tomato. Scatter the calamari over the mozzarella. Place in the oven for 3–5 minutes until cooked, turning to get an even colour. Remove and drizzle with a tablespoon of the reserved oil.

Makes one 30 cm (12 inch) pizza

RIGHT / An Amalfi Coast fisherman showing off a highly prized octopus.

Prawns, zucchini and mint

All great pizza begins with the best ingredients. This one has to have the best prawns you can find.

250 g (9 oz) ball of basic pizza dough (see pages 18–21), shaped (see pages 22–25)

2 tablespoons chopped fresh mint leaves
3 tablespoons extra virgin olive oil, plus extra for brushing
1 zucchini (courgette), trimmed and cut lengthways into 3 mm (⅛ inch) thick slices
Sea salt and freshly ground black pepper
150 g (5½ oz) fior di latte mozzarella
4–5 large king prawns (shrimp), shelled, deveined and sliced in half lengthways

TO ASSEMBLE / Marinate the chopped mint in the olive oil for an hour or so before making the pizza, then strain the leaves, keeping the oil. Season the zucchini, add a little extra virgin olive oil and chargrill for about 30 seconds on each side until tender.

Place a large tile in your oven for the pizza, then turn the oven up to preheat to full heat (without using any fan-forced function) for at least 20 minutes (see page 31). Thinly slice the mozzarella and scatter evenly, here and there, to top the shaped pizza base, leaving the edges clear to about 3–4 cm (1½ inches). Scatter the zucchini and prawn halves over the pizza so that each eventual pizza slice contains some. Place in the oven for 3–5 minutes until cooked, turning to get an even colour. Remove and drizzle with the mint oil.

Makes one 30 cm (12 inch) pizza

Hot calabrese

This pizza calls for a smoked cheese called provola and a typical Calabrese spreadable sausage called 'nduja. The Gaeta olive is a medium-sized black olive from south of Rome, renowned for its plump, meaty texture and excellent tart, salty flavour.

250 g (9 oz) ball of basic pizza dough (see pages 18–21), shaped (see pages 22–25)

2 best-quality Italian-style pork and fennel sausages
1 tablespoon 'nduja
100 g (3½ oz) smoked provola cheese
10 cherry tomatoes, halved
1 red or yellow capsicum (pepper), trimmed, deseeded and chopped into long strips
10 Gaeta (or similar) black olives, pitted
Sea salt
1 tablespoon extra virgin olive oil

TO ASSEMBLE / Place a large tile in your oven for the pizza, then turn the oven up to preheat to full heat (without using any fan-forced function) for at least 20 minutes (see page 31). Cut the skin and remove the meat from the sausages. Place in a bowl with the 'nduja. Mix well with hands or a fork. Thinly slice the smoked provola and scatter evenly, here and there, to top the shaped pizza base, leaving the edges clear to about 3–4 cm (1½ inches).

Add the sausage and 'nduja mixture evenly in dollops using a teaspoon. Finally, scatter the cherry tomatoes, capsicum slices and olives over the pizza. Season with a pinch of salt. Place the pizza in the oven for 3–5 minutes until cooked, turning to get an even colour. Remove and drizzle with the olive oil.

Makes one 30 cm (12 inch) pizza.

Gorgonzola, potato and radicchio

Most often it's the soft, delicate cheeses that are used on pizza, but when an assertive blue like gorgonzola is used, it dominates. The other ingredients support and complement. Potato is there for texture, radicchio as a flavour foil and rosemary binds the whole.

250 g (9 oz) ball of basic pizza
  dough (see pages 18–21), shaped
  (see pages 22–25)

100 g (3½ oz) fior di latte mozzarella
40 g (1½ oz/1 cup) radicchio leaves,
  sliced in 2 cm (¾ inch) wide strips
80 g (3 oz) gorgonzola cheese, cut
  into 12 pieces
12 very thin slices of potato (see note)
A pinch of sea salt
Freshly ground black pepper
1 teaspoon fresh young rosemary
  leaves

ROSEMARY OIL

2 tablespoons fresh young rosemary
  leaves
170 ml (5½ fl oz/⅔ cup) extra virgin
  olive oil

FOR THE ROSEMARY OIL / Finely chop the rosemary leaves with a very sharp knife. Place in a bowl and cover the leaves with the olive oil. Cover the bowl and place in a cool spot for 2 hours. Remove the leaves from the oil by passing through a fine sieve. Place the oil in a small squeezy bottle, ready to use. Any leftover oil can be kept in the refrigerator for up to a month.

TO ASSEMBLE / Place a large tile in your oven for the pizza, then turn the oven up to preheat to full heat (without using any fan-forced function) for at least 20 minutes (see page 31). Thinly slice the mozzarella and scatter evenly, here and there, to top the shaped pizza base, leaving the edges clear to about 3–4 cm (1½ inches). Scatter the radicchio and gorgonzola evenly over the pizza. Lay the potato slices on top. Season with a little salt, a couple of turns of the pepper mill and cook the pizza for 3–5 minutes until cooked, turning to get an even colour. Once out of the oven, drizzle with 1 tablespoon of the rosemary oil, scatter the rosemary leaves on top and serve.

Makes one 30 cm (12 inch) pizza

NOTE Use waxy, yellow-fleshed potatoes and to cut them very thin, use a mandolin or a food processor with a potato slicer. It's important that the potato slices are thin and see-through because they have to cook in a relatively short amount of time.

Roman pizza with tuna tartare

Raw seafood, called 'crudo' rather than 'carpaccio', is used by many of the protagonists in the 'new pizza' movement in Italy, both on the round wood-fired and the Roman teglia types. The seafood needs to be super fresh and the pizza consumed immediately.

1 sheet of Roman-style pizza dough (see pages 26–30), precooked (see page 31) and cut into 8 squares

2 teaspoons thinly sliced fresh chives

TUNA TARTARE
80 g (3 oz/½ cup) seedless raisins
800 g (1 lb 12 oz) tuna fillet, bloodline removed
8 anchovies, drained and finely chopped
80 g (3 oz/½ cup) pine nuts, toasted and roughly chopped
1 tablespoon Sicilian capers, soaked to desalt, chopped
6 tablespoons extra virgin olive oil
Sea salt and freshly ground black pepper

FOR THE TUNA TARTARE / Place the raisins in a bowl and cover with tepid water for 30 minutes. Drain and pat them dry. Meanwhile, cut the tuna carefully into 5 mm (¼ inch) cubes and place in a bowl. Chop the raisins and add to the tuna along with the anchovies, pine nuts, capers and olive oil. Mix well and season to taste with salt and pepper. Cover with plastic wrap and refrigerate for at least an hour.

TO ASSEMBLE / Place the Roman pizza squares on a baking tray and heat in a preheated 180°C (350°F) oven for about 5–6 minutes until they are crisp on the outside but soft in the middle. Meanwhile, remove the tuna tartare from the refrigerator. When the pizza squares are ready, remove from the oven, place on serving plates and evenly distribute the tuna tartare on top. Sprinkle with the sliced chives and finish by dressing with a little of the liquid left over from the tuna tartare.

Makes 8 squares

RIGHT / A Cetara fisherman mending his nets.

Roman pizza with crab, broad beans and chilli

It depends on the dish and the time of the season whether I double peel broad beans or not. Spring broad beans are tender and even their surrounding skin is edible (and occasionally the pod). It's only when summer temperatures start rising that this skin begins to thicken and become bitter. By that time the beans themselves turn mealy and pale and are best dried to store like other beans. The first peel is to take the outer pod off. The second is to then take the skin from each bean. It is the latter that takes time and many have no patience for this sort of job. If you can't be bothered or broad beans aren't available, tender spring peas work just as well. Certainly leaving broad beans unpeeled gives a dish robust flavour and texture.

1 sheet of Roman-style pizza dough
   (see pages 26–30)

300 g (10½ oz/1¼ cups) tinned San
   Marzano peeled tomatoes
2 tablespoons extra virgin olive oil
Sea salt and freshly ground black
   pepper
300 g (10½ oz) cooked crabmeat
3 tablespoons small fresh parsley
   leaves

BROAD BEAN AND CHILLI PUREE

370 g (13 oz/2 cups) 'double-peeled'
   broad beans
125 ml (4 fl oz/½ cup) extra virgin
   olive oil
2 red chillies, thinly sliced
6 tablespoons lemon juice

FOR THE BROAD BEAN AND CHILLI PUREE / Plunge the broad beans into boiling, salted water for 2 minutes until soft. Put three-quarters of the cooked, still warm, beans in a bowl with the olive oil and mash them with a fork until roughly puréed. Add the rest of the beans, chilli and lemon juice and season with salt and pepper to taste. Mix gently, keeping the whole broad beans intact.

TO ASSEMBLE / Preheat the oven to 220°C (425°F). Hand squeeze the tomatoes until they're uniformly mashed and mix in a tablespoon of extra virgin olive oil and a pinch of salt. Spread the tomato mixture on top of the pizza sheet as evenly as possible. If the dough has risen excessively, press down gently with the tips of your fingers to make small indentations to trap the tomato. Bake in the oven for 25 minutes. If the teglia is browning more on one side, your oven is not even and the tray may need to be turned. Once cooked, remove from the oven and let cool a little. Place on a serving plate as a large piece or cut into individual tiles. Spread the broad bean and chilli purée evenly over the pizza. Scatter with the crabmeat and then the parsley leaves and sprinkle with the remaining olive oil. Finish with a little freshly ground black pepper.

Serves 6–8

Chicory, salame and stracciatella

Chicory is native to the Mediterranean region and is widely used, raw and cooked, in various dishes. It is bitter, but cooking the green leaves removes much of the bitterness.

250 g (9 oz) ball of basic pizza
   dough (see pages 18–21), shaped
   (see pages 22–25)

100 g (3½ oz) fior di latte mozzarella
6 slices of good-quality Italian salame,
   sliced and cut into 'straws'
1 tablespoon grated parmesan cheese
4 tablespoons stracciatella cheese
A handful of confit tomatoes
   (see page 60)
1 tablespoon extra virgin olive oil
A couple of pinches of freshly ground
   black pepper

COOKED CHICORY

1 tablespoon salt
500 g (1 lb 2 oz) chicory leaves
1 tablespoon extra virgin olive oil
1 garlic clove, lightly crushed
Sea salt

FOR THE COOKED CHICORY / Bring 5 litres (175 fl oz/20 cups) of water to the boil in a pot with a tablespoon of salt added. Plunge in the chicory and submerge with a wooden spoon. After the water returns to the boil, cook the chicory for 3–4 minutes. Drain and let the leaves cool to room temperature. Squeeze as much water out of the leaves as possible. Place the chicory leaves on a board and roughly chop, then put in a bowl and add the olive oil, garlic clove and a little salt. Mix thoroughly. Any leftover chicory can be kept in the refrigerator for up to a week.

TO ASSEMBLE / Place a large tile in your oven for the pizza, then turn the oven up to preheat to full heat (without using any fan-forced function) for at least 20 minutes (see page 31). Thinly slice the mozzarella and scatter evenly, here and there, to top the shaped pizza base, leaving the edges clear to about 3–4 cm (1½ inches). Arrange the salame 'straws' on top and sprinkle over the grated parmesan. Place the pizza in the oven for 3–5 minutes until cooked, turning to get an even colour. Once out of the oven, arrange the chopped chicory over the pizza. Dollop the stracciatella on top and distribute the confit tomatoes over the lot. Drizzle with olive oil and add the pepper.

Makes one 30 cm (12 inch) pizza

Montasio, broccoli and prosciutto crackle

Montasio is a firm, flavoursome mountain cheese from the regions of Friuli and Veneto in northeastern Italy. When it melts, it adds a little bite to the broccoli cream. The fried prosciutto is added as a final crisp and salty note.

250 g (9 oz) ball of basic pizza dough (see pages 18–21), shaped (see pages 22–25)

3 large asparagus spears
80 g (3 oz) fior di latte mozzarella
1 tablespoon extra virgin olive oil
A pinch of sea salt
Freshly ground black pepper
60 g (2 oz) Montasio cheese, shaved using a potato peeler

PROSCIUTTO CRACKLE
80 ml (2½ fl oz/⅓ cup) extra virgin olive oil
8 thin slices of prosciutto

BROCCOLI CREAM
200 g (7 oz/3 cups) broccoli florets
3 tablespoons extra virgin olive oil
2–3 pinches of sea salt
A pinch of white pepper

FOR THE PROSCIUTTO CRACKLE / Heat the olive oil in a pan over medium–high heat and add the prosciutto slices, avoiding overlapping (that might mean frying only two or three at a time, depending on the pan size). After a minute or so, turn the prosciutto. When crisp, drain on a plate lined with paper towel. Leftovers can be stored in an airtight container lined with paper towel but don't store in the refrigerator.

FOR THE BROCCOLI CREAM / Blanch the broccoli florets in boiling water for 2 minutes and then drain well. Using a stick blender or food processor, blend with the olive oil, salt and pepper until smooth. Cool before using. Fill a piping bag with 4 tablespoons of the broccoli cream. Any left-over cream can be kept in the refrigerator for up to 5 days.

TO ASSEMBLE / Place a large tile in your oven and preheat to full heat (without using any fan-forced function) for at least 20 minutes (see page 31). Blanch the asparagus in boiling water for 20 seconds. Slice lengthways.

Thinly slice the mozzarella and scatter over the pizza base, leaving a clear edge of 3–4 cm (1½ inches). Arrange the asparagus over the mozzarella. Drizzle with olive oil. Season with a little salt and pepper and place in the oven for 3–5 minutes until cooked, turning to get an even colour. Scatter with the shaved Montasio and crush one or two rashers of prosciutto crackle over the top. Drop small blobs of the broccoli cream here and there before serving.

Makes one 30 cm (12 inch) pizza

Ceci – chickpeas, eggplant and salted ricotta

This pizza uses salted ricotta (ricotta salata), which is firm enough to grate and adds a salty, snow-like finish that looks and tastes wonderful. The chickpeas are puréed, adding flavour without their often mealy texture.

250 g (9 oz) ball of basic pizza dough (see pages 18–21), shaped (see pages 22–25)

100 g (3½ oz) fior di latte mozzarella
25 g (1 oz/¼ cup) thinly sliced leek
8–12 slices of chargrilled eggplant (aubergine) (see page 48)
A handful of confit tomatoes (see page 60)
1 tablespoon toasted pine nuts
2 tablespoons grated salted ricotta cheese

CHICKPEA PUREE

200 g (7 oz/1 cup) dried chickpeas
125 ml (4 fl oz/½ cup) extra virgin olive oil
1 garlic clove, crushed
A pinch of best-quality dried oregano
Salt and freshly ground black pepper

FOR THE CHICKPEA PUREE / Soak the chickpeas in abundant cold water for 24 hours. Drain well and wash the chickpeas to get rid of any skins that come off. Place in a pot and cover with cold water to a level of 6 cm (2½ inches) above the chickpeas. Bring the pot to the boil. Immediately turn down to a low simmer and cover with a lid. Keep simmering very gently for 2–3 hours until the chickpeas are soft and tender. Drain, but keep a cup of the cooking liquid. Place the cooked chickpeas in a blender with the olive oil, garlic and oregano. Pulse until smooth. Season to taste with salt and pepper. The purée should be thick enough to pipe. If it's too thick, add a little of the cooking water. Any left-over purée will keep for up to a week, covered, in the refrigerator.

TO ASSEMBLE / Place a large tile in your oven for the pizza, then turn the oven up to preheat to full heat (without using any fan-forced function) for at least 20 minutes (see page 31). Thinly slice the mozzarella and scatter evenly, here and there, to top the shaped pizza base, leaving the edges clear to about 3–4 cm (1½ inches). Scatter the leek and eggplant evenly over the pizza. Place the pizza in the oven for 3–5 minutes until cooked, turning to get an even colour. Once out of the oven, scatter with the confit tomatoes. Using a piping bag, pipe on the chickpea purée here and there, in dollops or strips, over the pizza. Add the pine nuts and salted ricotta.

Makes one 30 cm (12 inch) pizza

Roman pizza with cavolo nero, mushrooms and lardo

Lardo is the Italian word for pork back fat that has been salted, cured with herbs and spices and then dried. It must be mother-of-pearl white and smell and taste sweet. It should be sliced very thin and, when eaten, it should melt in the mouth.

1 sheet of Roman-style pizza dough
(see pages 26–30)

350 g (12 oz/1⅓ cups) tinned San
Marzano whole peeled tomatoes
1 tablespoon extra virgin olive oil
Pinch of salt
95 g (3½ oz/1 cup) parmesan
cheese shavings
32 thin slices of lardo

CAVOLO NERO AND MUSHROOMS

20 g (¾ oz) dried porcini mushrooms
500 g (1 lb 2 oz) cavolo nero,
stems removed
3 tablespoons extra virgin olive oil
2 garlic cloves, crushed
1 small white onion, finely chopped
300 g (10½ oz) button or Swiss
brown mushrooms, sliced
150 g (5½ oz) shiitake mushrooms,
sliced
3 tablespoons chopped fresh parsley
Sea salt and freshly ground black
pepper

FOR THE CAVOLO NERO AND MUSHROOMS / First soak the dried porcini in a small bowl of cold water for 10–15 minutes until soft. Drain and chop them. Bring a pot of water to a rolling boil and blanch the cavolo nero leaves for 90 seconds. Drain well. Heat 2 tablespoons of the oil in a pan and gently fry the garlic and onion together for a minute. Add the mushrooms and fry over a medium heat, constantly stirring, until they have softened. Add the parsley and cavolo nero, season to taste with salt and pepper and stir well. After simmering for a moment more, turn off the heat. Any left-over mixture can be refrigerated for 3–4 days. (If reheating to use on the pizza, make sure the mixture is hot, or at least warm, to melt the lardo slightly.)

TO ASSEMBLE / Preheat the oven to 220°C (425°F). Hand squeeze the tomatoes until they're uniformly mashed and mix in the extra virgin olive oil and a pinch of salt. Spread the tomato mixture on top of the sheet of pizza as evenly as possible. If the dough has risen excessively, press down gently with the tips of your fingers to make small indentations to trap the tomato. Bake in the oven for 25 minutes. If the teglia is browning more on one side, your oven is not even and the tray may need to be turned. Once cooked, remove from the oven and let cool a little. Place on a serving plate as a large piece or cut, using scissors, into individual tiles. Spread the warm–hot cavolo nero and mushroom mixture evenly over the pizza. Scatter the shavings of parmesan across the top and finally drape the lardo slices over. The heat of the mixture will melt the lardo a little, so it becomes transparent. Serve immediately.

Serves 6–8

Capocollo, pickled red onion and pecorino

Capocollo is cured pork neck. Use a semi-hard pecorino cheese, rather than a firm, grating style. The pickled red onion recipe makes enough for 6 pizze. Any extra can be served as an accompaniment to grilled meats or seafood or used as an addition to summer salads.

250 g (9 oz) ball of basic pizza dough (see pages 18–21), shaped (see pages 22–25)

100 g (3½ oz) fior di latte mozzarella
12 thin slices of capocollo di Martina Franca
60 g (2 oz/¾ cup) pecorino cheese shavings
Freshly ground black pepper

PICKLED RED ONION

4 large red onions, halved and thinly sliced
250 ml (9 fl oz/1 cup) red wine vinegar
50 g (2 oz/¼ cup) sugar
125 ml (4 fl oz/½ cup) water
2 tablespoons extra virgin olive oil
1 tablespoon finely chopped fresh parsley
Sea salt and freshly ground black pepper

FOR THE PICKLED RED ONION / Place the sliced onion in a wide, shallow, preferably ceramic dish. Bring the vinegar, sugar and water to the boil in a saucepan and immediately pour the boiling liquid onto the onion. Let cool to room temperature. The onion is now ready to be drained and used or stored in its liquid – it will become tastier over a few days. To serve, drain and squeeze out the vinegar, dress with extra virgin olive oil and the parsley and season. Pickled onions can be stored in their liquid, in the refrigerator, for up to a month.

TO ASSEMBLE / Place a large tile in your oven for the pizza, then turn the oven up to preheat to full heat (without using any fan-forced function) for at least 20 minutes (see page 31). Thinly slice the mozzarella and scatter evenly, here and there, to top the shaped pizza base, leaving the edges clear to about 3–4 cm (1½ inches). Place the pizza in the oven for 3–5 minutes until cooked, turning to get an even colour. Once cooked, place the capocollo slices over the cooked pizza and scatter the shaved pecorino on top with a few grinds of black pepper. Finally, scatter 3 tablespoons of the pickled red onion over the top.

Makes one 30 cm (12 inch) pizza

Pork and fennel sausage, artichoke, buffalo ricotta

I've taken the filling out of the sausage casings for good reason. If the sausage is merely sliced, the casings can have the texture of rubber bands when cooked quickly at high heat. It's also easier to distribute the sausage evenly on the pizza. If fresh artichokes aren't available, there are good Italian artichokes in oil available at specialist stores.

250 g (9 oz) ball of basic pizza dough (see pages 18–21), shaped (see pages 22–25)

120 g (4¼ oz) fior di latte mozzarella, thinly sliced

3 cooked artichokes (see note), cut into quarters

40 g (1½ oz/¾ cup) grated parmesan cheese

140 g (5 oz) best-quality Italian-style pork and fennel sausages, meat removed from casings

Sea salt

80 g (3 oz/⅓ cup) buffalo milk ricotta cheese

8–10 fennel fronds

TOMATO FILLETS

1 kg (2 lb 4 oz) ripe tomatoes
Sea salt

FOR THE TOMATO FILLETS / Plunge the tomatoes into boiling salted water for 20–30 seconds, then plunge into iced water. After 5 minutes, they'll peel easily. Peel, halve and scoop out all seeds with a spoon. Cut each half in two, then each quarter into fillets. Unused fillets will keep for 2–3 days, refrigerated.

TO ASSEMBLE / Place a large tile in your oven for the pizza, then turn the oven up to preheat to full heat (without using any fan-forced function) for at least 20 minutes (see page 31). Scatter mozzarella over the pizza base, leaving the edges clear to about 3–4 cm (1½ inches). Distribute the artichoke quarters and tomato fillets over the top. Sprinkle with parmesan and sausage meat. Season with salt and place in the oven for 3–5 minutes until cooked, turning for even colour. Once out of the oven, use a teaspoon to place small blobs of buffalo ricotta here and there. Finally, place the fennel fronds evenly over the top.

Makes one 30 cm (12 inch) pizza

NOTE / Choose firm, unblemished artichokes. With a paring knife, take the top 2–3 cm (1 inch) off each artichoke, then pare around the heart until you reach the tender inner leaves. Leave about 4–5 cm (2 inches) of stalk at the base and trim away any leaves. As each artichoke is prepared, place in a pan of cold water with lemon juice added – weight them down with a plate so they sit in the lemon water and don't discolour. Bring to the boil, then simmer for 10–15 minutes until tender with a hint of resistance. Drain and cool completely. Use within 3–4 days or store in jars in olive oil for up to 14 days in the fridge.

OPPOSITE / Wild fennel flowers and pollen on the Alta Murgia in Puglia. **THIS PAGE** / Afternoons in Altamura, Puglia.

Roman pizza filled with cavolo nero frittata and 'nduja

When my brother and I would come home from school or after playing all day, my mother would make a frittata in what seemed like an instant. It was her quick fix for two hungry boys. As I grew up, my friends at school would have their egg sandwiches and I had my frittata sandwich. This recalls that very sandwich, with the grown-up addition of spicy 'nduja. Cavolo nero is also called Tuscan black kale. Tender spinach leaves can be substituted.

1 sheet of Roman-style pizza dough (see pages 26–30), precooked (see page 31) and cut into 8 squares

4 tablespoons 'nduja
70 g (2½ oz/2 cups) young rocket (arugula) leaves, trimmed
2 tablespoons extra virgin olive oil

CAVOLO NERO FRITTATA
4 large leaves of cavolo nero, stems removed
12 large eggs
Sea salt and freshly ground black pepper
4 tablespoons grated parmesan cheese
2 tablespoons chopped fresh parsley
4 tablespoons extra virgin olive oil
2 small leeks, washed thoroughly and cut into thin rounds
2 garlic cloves, crushed

FOR THE CAVOLO NERO FRITTATA / Bring a pot of water to the boil and plunge in the trimmed cavolo nero leaves. Boil for 3 minutes, then drain and let cool. Chop the leaves. Crack the eggs into a bowl. Add salt and pepper, beat lightly, then add the parmesan, chopped parsley and the cavolo nero. Beat lightly to mix the ingredients. Heat half the olive oil in a pan and lightly fry half the leek and garlic until soft. This should take about 2 minutes. Add half the egg mixture to the pan. Lift the edges as it cooks and firms up with a spatula. Keep doing this for about 90 seconds on a medium–high heat. Turn the frittata and cook the other side for a minute or so until the middle feels firm to the touch. Allow the frittata to cool in the pan before repeating with the remaining ingredients to make a second.

TO ASSEMBLE / Cut each pizza square in half, opening it to form a 'sandwich'. Place the halves back together on a baking tray and heat in a preheated 180°C (350°F) oven for about 5–6 minutes until they are crisp on the outside but soft in the middle. Once ready, remove from the oven. Spread a little 'nduja on the underside of the top half of each square. Place the bottom halves on serving plates or wooden boards and first place some rocket leaves on top, then a quarter of a frittata. Sprinkle with extra virgin olive oil and close with the top half of the square.

Makes 8 filled Roman pizze

Roman pizza with silverbeet, field mushrooms and fontina

Silverbeet, or Swiss chard, prepared in this combination with mushrooms and fontina is a dish that I enjoy on steaming polenta. And when the silverbeet is young and tender, the stalks are excellent for the texture as well as the bittersweet flavour they impart. Choose large, meaty mushrooms for this. They should feel heavy in your hand. If you can get fresh porcini mushrooms, all the better.

1 sheet of Roman-style pizza dough (see pages 26–30), precooked (see page 31) and left whole or cut into 8 squares

300 g (10½ oz) fontina cheese, thinly sliced
2 tablespoons grated parmesan
2 tablespoons chopped fresh parsley
2 tablespoons extra virgin olive oil

BRAISED SILVERBEET
12 young silverbeet (Swiss chard) leaves, stems intact
2 tablespoons extra virgin olive oil
1 garlic clove, crushed, in one piece
80 ml (2½ fl oz/⅓ cup) dry white wine
Sea salt and black pepper

PAN-FRIED FIELD MUSHROOMS
3–4 tablespoons extra virgin olive oil
6–8 large field mushrooms, cut into 1 cm (½ inch) thick slices

FOR THE BRAISED SILVERBEET / Fill a large pot three-quarters full of water. Add a teaspoon of salt, cover, and bring to the boil. Meanwhile, trim off the bottoms of the silverbeet stems and wash well. Plunge into the boiling water and keep submerged using a wooden spoon. Once the water boils again, simmer for 2 minutes. Drain well. In a wide braising pan, heat the oil and add the garlic. When it begins to fry, add the silverbeet and move the leaves around carefully in the pan for 1 minute, keeping the leaves intact. Add the wine and cook until the liquid has disappeared. Season with salt and pepper and place aside to cool. Any left-over silverbeet can be refrigerated for 2–3 days.

FOR THE PAN-FRIED FIELD MUSHROOMS / Heat 2 tablespoons olive oil in a wide pan. Once the oil begins to smoke, place the mushroom slices in carefully, in batches if necessary. After 20–30 seconds, turn them to cook on the other side for 10–15 seconds. Place on a plate covered with paper towel and season lightly with salt. Heat more oil, as needed, and repeat with the remaining mushrooms. Any left-over mushrooms can be refrigerated for 2–3 days.

TO ASSEMBLE / Place the Roman pizza sheet or squares on a baking tray. Distribute the fontina slices on top and sprinkle with the parmesan. Evenly spread the silverbeet on top, then the mushrooms and bake in a preheated 180°C (350°F) oven for 10 minutes. Sprinkle with the parsley and finish with extra virgin olive oil before cutting into pieces to serve.

Makes 8 squares

Fried pizza with scarola and crabmeat

The idea for this fried pizza came from a dish by Enzo Coccia, who devised it after reading Ippolito Cavalcanti's 1837 manuscript Cucina Teorico-Pratica. *Scarola is an endive (Cichorium endivia), which is harvested in autumn through to early spring. It's popular in Italy either raw or cooked. This recipe is for two fried pizze, but it's always best to make a lot more while the oil is hot.*

250 g (9 oz) ball of basic pizza
    dough (see pages 18–21)

160 g (5½ oz) cooked crabmeat
1 teaspoon colatura d'alici
Extra virgin olive oil or peanut oil,
    for frying

FRIED SCAROLA
3–4 heads of scarola, washed well
2 tablespoons extra virgin olive oil
1 garlic clove, crushed
10 Gaeta (or similar) black olives,
    pitted and quartered
2 tablespoons sultanas (golden raisins)
60 ml (2 fl oz/¼ cup) dry white wine
3 tablespoons toasted pine nuts
Sea salt and freshly ground black
    pepper

FOR THE FRIED SCAROLA / Divide the scarola into individual leaves. Heat the olive oil in a wide frying pan and fry the garlic and olives for a minute, making sure the garlic does not colour. Add the scarola and sultanas and mix for 30 seconds until the leaves have softened a little. Add the wine and turn up the heat to evaporate the liquid. Cover the pan, turn the heat to low, and cook for 2–3 minutes. Remove the lid, add the toasted pine nuts, season with salt and pepper to taste, mix, and cook off any liquid. Remove from heat, and let the mixture cool completely before using for the fried pizze. This makes enough for 8–10 pizze.

TO ASSEMBLE / Divide the dough ball in two. Prepare the pizza discs as you would for normal pizza, but make the discs around 16–18 cm (6–7 inches) wide and don't leave the cornice on the border (see pages 22–25). As the discs are going to be folded in half, divide about a quarter of the fried scarola mixture evenly between the bottom half of each disc and spread it out to about 3 cm (1¼ inches) from the bottom and 5–6 cm (2–2½ inches) from the sides. Scatter the crabmeat on top and sprinkle each with ½ teaspoon of colatura d'alici. Fold each disc to enclose the stuffing and lightly pinch the borders to seal them. Choose a wide pot or deep-fryer to contain the stuffed pizza. Heat the oil to 175°C (350°F) at a depth of at least 4–5 cm (1½–2 inches), then place the pizze carefully in, one at a time, and fry until crisp and golden. They will need to be moved constantly and turned so that they are golden on both sides. Remove with a slotted spoon or 'spider' and drain on paper towel. Serve hot.

Makes 2 fried pizze

Roman pizza with roast garlic, tomato and olives

This is such a simple combination of great ingredients. When garlic is roasted it loses much of its aggressive flavour: it is tamed into a smoky, sweet paste that can be used in many preparations.

1 sheet of Roman-style pizza dough
(see pages 26–30)

350 g (12 oz/1⅓ cups) tinned San
Marzano whole peeled tomatoes
1 tablespoon extra virgin olive oil
Pinch of sea salt
16 slices of fior di latte mozzarella

ROAST GARLIC, TOMATO AND OLIVES

4 whole bulbs of garlic
150 g (5½ oz/1 cup) large black
olives, pitted and roughly chopped
500 g (1 lb 2 oz) assorted small
tomatoes – baby roma (plum),
yellow teardrop, cherry, cut in half
1 sprig of fresh thyme
1 sprig of fresh oregano
1 tablespoon chopped fresh parsley
2 tablespoons extra virgin olive oil
1 tablespoon red wine vinegar
Sea salt and freshly ground black
pepper

FOR THE ROAST GARLIC, TOMATO AND OLIVES / Preheat the oven to 160°C (320°F). Place the whole, unpeeled garlic bulbs on a roasting tray or pan and roast for 20 minutes. When ready, the cloves should be soft. Cool a little until they are comfortable to handle and peel each clove, then cut it in half. Place the peeled cloves in a bowl with the chopped olives and tomato halves. Remove the leaves from the sprigs of thyme and oregano and add to the bowl along with the parsley, olive oil and vinegar. Season with salt and pepper to taste and mix well. Any left-over roast tomatoes can be refrigerated for a week.

TO ASSEMBLE / Preheat the oven to 220°C (425°F). Hand squeeze the tomatoes until they're uniformly mashed and mix in the extra virgin olive oil and a pinch of salt. Spread the tomato mixture on top of the sheet of pizza as evenly as possible. If the dough has risen excessively, press down gently with the tips of your fingers to make small indentations to trap the tomato. Bake in the oven for 25 minutes. If the teglia is browning more on one side, your oven is not even and the tray may need to be turned. Once cooked, remove from the oven and let cool a little. Place on a serving plate as a large piece or cut, using scissors, into individual tiles. Begin to dress the pizza by putting two slices of mozzarella on each tile first. Next, scatter with a tablespoon of the roast garlic, tomato and olive mixture for each tile and finish by sprinkling with some of the dressing left in the bowl.

Serves 6–8

RIGHT / Tomatoes from Cetara, on the Amalfi Coast.

Roman pizza with lentils, cauliflower and two cheeses

Braised lentils with cauliflower and cheese is one of my winter standards. The combination of sweet gruyère and tangy Parmigiano Reggiano is the essential element that binds the lot.

1 sheet of Roman-style pizza dough
(see pages 26–30)

1 medium-sized head of cauliflower
150 g (5½ oz/1½ cups) gruyère
cheese, grated
150 g (5½ oz/1½ cups) parmesan
cheese, grated
2 tablespoons extra virgin olive oil
3 tablespoons chopped fresh parsley

BRAISED LENTILS

3 tablespoons extra virgin olive oil
½ celery heart, finely chopped
1 small carrot, finely chopped
1 small onion, finely chopped
1 small leek, washed thoroughly and
sliced into 5 mm (¼ inch) half rounds
1 sprig of fresh rosemary, chopped
1 sprig of fresh thyme, chopped
100 g (3½ oz/½ cup) lentils, washed
150 g (5½ oz/⅔ cup) tinned San
Marzano whole peeled tomatoes
2 garlic cloves, crushed
30 g (1 oz/1 cup) roughly chopped
fresh flat-leaf parsley

FOR THE BRAISED LENTILS / In a braising pan, lightly fry the vegetables in the extra virgin olive oil until they soften, without colouring them. Add the chopped rosemary and thyme and continue to fry for a minute, stirring. Add the lentils and stir. Add the tomatoes and enough water to just cover the lentils. Cook for 40–60 minutes until the lentils are tender, adding more water if necessary. When the lentils are cooked, stir in the crushed garlic, parsley and seasoning. Cool until needed. Any left-over lentils can be refrigerated for up to a week.

TO ASSEMBLE / Poach (or steam) the whole cauliflower in boiling water or a steamer until tender. A skewer, or the point of a sharp knife, should be able to pierce the stalk with only a little resistance. Remove from the water or steamer and set aside to cool, then slice 2 cm (¾ inch) thick slices from top to bottom. Cut into small, bite-sized pieces and place between clean dish towels, patting completely dry. Preheat the oven to 220°C (425°F). Take the sheet of pizza and if the dough has risen excessively, press down gently with the tips of your fingers to make small indentations on the surface of the dough. Spread the cooked cauliflower pieces on top of the dough as evenly as possible. Season with a few pinches of salt and some freshly ground pepper. Mix the cheeses together and sprinkle evenly over the cauliflower. Bake in the oven for 25 minutes. If the teglia is browning more on one side, your oven is not even and the tray may need to be turned. Once cooked, remove from the oven and rest for 2–3 minutes. Place on a serving plate as a large piece or cut into individual tiles. Dollop about a cupful of the heated braised lentils here and there with a spoon and sprinkle with the olive oil. Finish with the chopped parsley.

Serves 6–8

Roman pizza with cuttlefish, broccoli and chilli

Cuttlefish is often seen as a poor version of calamari (squid). In truth they are very different and both equally delicious. Cuttlefish is thicker, meatier and more pronounced in flavour. It matches and complements the bold flavours in this dish, especially with the addition of the colatura d'alici (anchovy sauce).

1 sheet of Roman-style pizza dough
(see pages 26–30)

350 g (12 oz/1⅓ cups) tinned San
Marzano whole peeled tomatoes
2 tablespoons extra virgin olive oil
500 g (1 lb 2 oz) cleaned cuttlefish,
cut into 1 cm (½ inch) wide strips
2 red chillies, sliced
1 teaspoon colatura d'alici

PAN-FRIED BROCCOLI
600 g (1 lb 5 oz) broccoli, trimmed
of woody stalks
3 tablespoons extra virgin olive oil
1 onion, finely diced
2 garlic cloves, crushed
Sea salt and freshly ground black
pepper

FOR THE PAN-FRIED BROCCOLI / Cut the broccoli heads into florets and stalks into 1 cm (½ inch) lengths. Bring a pot of water to a rolling boil and blanch the broccoli for 90 seconds. Drain well. Heat the olive oil in a large pan and gently fry the onion and garlic until soft. Turn the heat up to moderate and add the broccoli, stirring constantly for about 4 minutes until tender. Season with a couple of good pinches of salt and a little ground pepper.

TO ASSEMBLE / Preheat the oven to 220°C (425°F). Hand squeeze the tomatoes until they're uniformly mashed and mix in a tablespoon of extra virgin olive oil and a pinch of salt. Spread the tomato mixture on top of the dough as evenly as possible. If the dough has risen excessively, press down gently with the tips of your fingers to make small indentations to trap the tomato. Bake in the oven for 25 minutes. If the teglia is browning more on one side, your oven is not even and the tray may need to be turned. While the pizza is cooking, heat the remaining olive oil in a wide heavy-based frying pan. Once the oil begins to smoke, carefully add the cuttlefish and chilli and cook quickly for a minute or so, continually moving them in the pan. Once the teglia sheet is cooked, remove from the oven and let cool a little. Place on a serving plate as a large piece or cut, using scissors, into individual tiles. Scatter with the pan-fried broccoli and the fried cuttlefish. Mix the colatura d'alici with 125 ml (4 fl oz) of the cuttlefish cooking juices and spoon over the top as a final dressing.

Serves 6–8

Roman pizza with potato, calamari, spinach and chilli

With a base of potato cooked on this bubbly Roman pizza dough, almost anything will taste good as a topping. Any alternative braised vegetable could just as easily sit here, such as asparagus, artichokes or winter greens.

1 sheet of Roman-style pizza dough (see pages 26–30)

500 g (1 lb 2 oz) yellow-fleshed waxy potatoes such as Spunta, Nicola or Desiree
2 tablespoons extra virgin olive oil
Sea salt and freshly ground black pepper

CALAMARI, SPINACH AND CHILLI
300 g (10½ oz) English spinach, washed well
2 French shallots, thinly sliced
2 garlic cloves, crushed
2 red chillies, sliced
3 tablespoons extra virgin olive oil
800 g (1 lb 12 oz) cleaned calamari (squid), patted dry and thinly sliced
Sea salt and freshly ground black pepper

FOR THE CALAMARI, SPINACH AND CHILLI / Bring a pot of salted water to the boil and plunge in the spinach. Boil for 2 minutes, submerging with a wooden spoon, then drain and cool. Wring the spinach well with your hands to remove as much water as possible. Place on a board and chop roughly. Fry the shallots, garlic and chillies in 2 tablespoons of the olive oil until soft. Add the spinach and stir for 3 minutes, then remove from the heat. In another pan, heat the remaining olive oil on a high flame and fry the calamari for 30–40 seconds, stirring constantly. Add it to the spinach, season with salt and pepper and mix well. Let it come to room temperature. If there is a lot of liquid, drain it off before using on the pizza. Any left-over calamari can be refrigerated for 3–4 days.

TO ASSEMBLE / Scrub the potatoes clean. Place in a pot of water, then cover the pot with a lid and boil. Simmer, and keep cooking until the potatoes are soft. A skewer should easily pierce the potatoes all the way to the centre. Remove from the heat, drain and cool. Peel the potatoes and break the flesh apart with your fingers. Place in a bowl and mix with the extra virgin olive oil and the salt and pepper. Preheat the oven to 220°C (425°F). Evenly spread the potatoes on top of the sheet of pizza. If the dough has risen excessively, press down gently with the tips of your fingers to make small indentations. Bake for 25 minutes. If the teglia is browning more on one side, turn the oven tray to spread heat evenly. Once cooked, remove from the oven and let cool a little. Place on a serving plate as a large piece or cut, using scissors, into individual tiles. Distribute the drained calamari, spinach and chilli mixture evenly over the potatoes.

Serves 6–8

RIGHT / The seaside town of Cetara.

Frutti di mare (seafood) and avocado

Many people believe that a seafood pizza is a 'Marinara'. It's not. A Marinara pizza is the simplest of all pizze with tomato, garlic, oregano and extra virgin olive oil. A seafood pizza is a 'Frutti di mare'. We have a version of this seafood pizza on the menu at all times.

250 g (9 oz) ball of basic pizza
   dough (see pages 18–21), shaped
   (see pages 22–25)

3 large scallops, halved
3 large king prawns (shrimp), shelled,
   deveined and sliced in half
   lengthways
70 g (2½ oz) cleaned calamari
   (squid), sliced into 5 x 1 cm
   (2 x ½ inch) pieces, patted dry
   with paper towel
1 tablespoon extra virgin olive oil,
   plus 1 teaspoon for the avocado
1 garlic clove, crushed
Sea salt and freshly ground black
   pepper
½ avocado, flesh removed
Juice of 1 lime
2 tablespoons chopped fresh parsley
100 g (3½ oz) fior di latte mozzarella
10 cherry tomatoes, quartered

TO ASSEMBLE / Place a large tile in your oven for the pizza, then turn the oven up to preheat to full heat (without using any fan-forced function) for at least 20 minutes (see page 31).

Prepare all the seafood first so it is ready to go on your pizza. Scallops and prawns can go on raw as they will cook quickly on the pizza. The calamari needs to be cooked briefly first by heating a tablespoon of extra virgin olive oil in a small heavy-based frying pan and tossing the calamari in over a high heat with the crushed garlic. Season with salt and pepper and fry for about 30 seconds. Remove from the pan into a cold bowl with all the juices. Place the avocado flesh in a small bowl with the lime juice, half the parsley, a pinch of salt and pepper and a teaspoon of extra virgin olive oil. Mash with a fork until smooth. Place in a piping bag in the refrigerator.

Thinly slice the mozzarella and scatter evenly, here and there, to top the shaped pizza base, leaving the edges clear to about 3–4 cm (1½ inches). Scatter the seafood over the mozzarella, reserving the oil from the cooked calamari. Distribute the tomato quarters over the surface. Place the pizza in the oven for 3–5 minutes until cooked, turning to get an even colour. Remove, drizzle the calamari oil on top and pipe a little avocado next to each of the six slices of scallop. Finish by scattering the rest of the parsley on top.

Makes one 30 cm (12 inch) pizza

Roman pizza with baba ganoush and prawns

Baba ganoush is the famous Middle Eastern preparation made from eggplant (aubergine), sesame paste (tahini), garlic and olive oil. I make it regularly to spread on crusty bread with countless other things on top. In this case it's being served with prawns (shrimp), but it would go just as well with scallops, octopus or lamb shoulder.

1 sheet of Roman-style pizza dough (see pages 26–30)

350 g (12 oz/1⅓ cups) tinned San Marzano whole peeled tomatoes
2 tablespoons extra virgin olive oil
Sea salt
32 medium prawns (shrimp), shelled
2 tablespoons finely chopped fresh parsley

BABA GANOUSH
3 large eggplants (aubergines)
2 tablespoons tahini
2 tablespoons lemon juice
2 garlic cloves
Sea salt
2 tablespoons extra virgin olive oil
1 teaspoon smoked paprika
1 tablespoon finely chopped fresh flat-leaf parsley

FOR THE BABA GANOUSH / Place each eggplant over a gas flame, turning until the skin is evenly charred and the flesh is soft all the way to the centre. Remove and cool for 10–15 minutes. Cut the eggplants in half, top to bottom, scoop out the flesh and place in a colander to drain for 15–20 minutes. Place the eggplant in a food processor with the tahini, lemon juice, garlic and salt and process until smooth. Add extra tahini, lemon juice or salt to taste. Spoon into a bowl and add the olive oil so it covers the top. Sprinkle the smoked paprika and parsley over. Any left-over baba ganoush can be refrigerated for 3–4 days.

TO ASSEMBLE / Preheat the oven to 220°C (425°F). Hand squeeze the tomatoes until they're uniformly mashed. Mix in a tablespoon of olive oil and a pinch of salt. Spread the tomato mixture over the sheet of pizza as evenly as possible. If the dough has risen excessively, press down gently with the tips of your fingers to make small indentations to trap the tomato. Bake in the oven for 25 minutes. If the teglia is browning more on one side, turn the oven tray to spread heat evenly. While the teglia is cooking, heat the remaining olive oil in a pan. When it begins to smoke, add half the prawns and fry until just cooked. Remove the cooked prawns and season with salt. Fry the remaining prawns the same way. Reserve any cooking juices. Once the teglia is cooked, remove from the oven and let cool a little. Spoon baba ganoush over the surface, then place the prawns on top. Scatter with the parsley and sprinkle the prawn cooking juices over the lot. Serve as a large piece or cut, using scissors, into individual tiles.

Serves 6–8

OPPOSITE / Card games are a popular pastime on sunny days in Cetara. **THIS PAGE** / Fishing boats moored off Cetara.

Roman pizza with potato and braised beef cheeks

Here's a pizza for the cold days of winter when we long for slow-cooked, gelatinous dishes such as osso buco and oxtail. These beef cheeks have a good deal of pepper in their preparation and, combined with the potato on top of a crisp and airy pizza tile, they become a complete dish.

1 sheet of Roman-style pizza dough (see pages 26–30)

500 g (1 lb 2 oz) yellow-fleshed waxy potatoes, such as Spunta, Nicola or Desiree
2 tablespoons extra virgin olive oil
2 tablespoons chopped fresh parsley

BRAISED PEPPERED BEEF CHEEKS
2 kg (4 lb 8 oz) beef cheeks, cut into 2 cm (¾ inch) cubes
4 garlic cloves, lightly crushed
1 red onion, cut into 1 cm (½ inch) cubes
1 carrot, cut into 1 cm (½ inch) cubes
2 celery stalks, cut into 1 cm (½ inch) cubes
1 litre (35 fl oz/4 cups) dry red wine
1 tablespoon freshly ground black pepper
1 tablespoon tomato paste (concentrated puree)
2 bay leaves
500 ml (17 fl oz/2 cups) veal stock

FOR THE BRAISED PEPPERED BEEF CHEEKS / Place the cubed beef in a casserole dish with the garlic, onion, carrot, celery and enough wine to just cover the meat. Bring to a simmer and keep simmering for 2 hours, partly covered with a lid. Add the pepper, tomato paste, bay leaves, the rest of the wine and the veal stock. Add two to three good pinches of salt and stir in. Keep simmering gently, uncovered, for 2 or more hours until the sauce has reduced and thickened. If it dries out too much and catches on the bottom, stir in a little more stock. When cooked, check the seasoning and add a little more salt, if needed. Any left-over beef cheeks can be frozen or refrigerated for up to 6 days.

TO ASSEMBLE / Scrub the potatoes clean. Place in a pot of water, then cover the pot with a lid and boil. Simmer, and keep cooking until the potatoes are soft. A skewer should easily pierce the potatoes all the way to the centre. Remove from the heat, drain and cool. Peel the potatoes and break the flesh apart with your fingers. Place in a bowl and mix with the extra virgin olive oil and some salt. Preheat the oven to 220°C (425°F). Spread the potatoes on top of the sheet of pizza as evenly as possible. If the dough has risen excessively, press down gently with the tips of your fingers to make small indentations. Bake in the oven for 25 minutes. If the teglia is browning more on one side, your oven is not even and the tray may need to be turned. Once cooked, remove from the oven and let cool a little. Cut into eight individual tiles and place on serving plates. Distribute about half the warm braised beef cheeks here and there, over the potatoes, spooning a little of the sauce on top. Sprinkle with the parsley.

Makes 8 squares

Lamb belly, ricotta and Mediterranean herbs

This pizza has become somewhat of a Pizzaperta signature. We put it on the menu when lamb is at its best, approaching spring and early summer. It can be done exactly the same way using kid goat or pork belly. A typical lamb belly will weigh between 600–800 g (1 lb 5 oz–1 lb 12 oz). It will shrink slightly once cooked, but if you choose two bellies within these weight parameters, there should be enough to make six or more pizze.

250 g (9 oz) ball of basic pizza
    dough (see pages 18–21), shaped
    (see pages 22–25)

80 g (3 oz/⅓ cup) ricotta cheese
40 g (1½ oz/½ cup) grated parmesan
100 g (3½ oz) fior di latte mozzarella
6 tomato fillets (see page 102)
1 tablespoon Mediterranean herbs
    – rosemary, sage, thyme, oregano
    and marjoram, finely chopped

SLOW-COOKED LAMB BELLY

1.2 kg (2 lb 10 oz) lamb belly,
    trimmed of any excess fat
1 carrot, in 1 cm (½ inch) rounds
1 celery stalk, in 1 cm (½ inch) slices
2 garlic cloves, peeled and left whole
1 small onion, chopped
2 bay leaves
8 peppercorns
1–2 litres (35–70 fl oz/4–8 cups)
    lamb or chicken stock

FOR THE SLOW-COOKED LAMB BELLY / Preheat the oven to 140°C (275°F). Place the lamb bellies side by side, not overlapping, in an oven dish. Place all the vegetables, bay leaves and peppercorns around. Pour in the stock and make sure the meat is covered by at least 1 cm (½ inch) of liquid, increasing the quantity if necessary. Cover the dish tightly with foil and place in the oven for 4 hours. After this time, pierce the meat with a skewer – if it pierces easily, it is done. If not, leave it in longer. Once cooked, remove the meat from the liquid and let it cool. (You can reuse the liquid for stock, by draining the vegetables, skimming off the fat, and refrigerating or freezing.) Place the cool lamb belly on a dish and place a weight on top to keep its thickness uniform. Refrigerate overnight. Any left-over lamb belly will keep for up to 5 days, refrigerated.

TO ASSEMBLE / Place a large tile in your oven for the pizza, then preheat at full heat (without using any fan-forced function) for at least 20 minutes (see page 31). Cut about a sixth of the lamb into 12 thin rectangles. Mix the ricotta and parmesan together and place in a piping bag. Thinly slice the mozzarella and scatter to top the pizza base, leaving the edges clear to 3–4 cm (1½ inches). Place the tomato fillets across the top. Distribute the lamb pieces over the pizza and season. Place the pizza into the oven for 3–5 minutes until cooked, turning to get an even colour. Once out of the oven, pipe blobs of the ricotta and parmesan mixture over the cooked pizza and sprinkle with the chopped herbs.

Makes one 30 cm (12 inch) pizza

Roman pizza with broccoli, marinated anchovies and capers

These are flavours of southern Italy, where vegetables are given their due respect. The anchovies used are filleted and marinated in a little brine and vinegar – not too much – so their flavours are maintained.

1 sheet of Roman-style pizza dough
(see pages 26–30)

400 g (14 oz) fior di latte mozzarella,
thinly sliced
2 tablespoons grated parmesan
cheese
1 teaspoon best-quality dried oregano
40 marinated 'white' anchovies
Confit tomatoes (see page 60)
16 caper leaves (optional)
2 tablespoons extra virgin olive oil

COOKED BROCCOLI

1 kg (2 lb 4 oz) broccoli, trimmed of
any tough stalks
2 tablespoons extra virgin olive oil
Sea salt and freshly ground black
pepper

FRIED CAPERS

160 g (5½ oz/1 cup) Sicilian capers,
soaked to desalt
250 ml (9 fl oz/1 cup) extra virgin
olive oil

COOKED BROCCOLI / Bring a large pot, two-thirds filled with water, to the boil. Plunge in the broccoli and cook for 5 minutes. Drain and let the broccoli cool. Chop roughly and place in a bowl. Add the olive oil and season to taste with salt and pepper. Any left-over broccoli can be refrigerated for up to a week.

FOR THE FRIED CAPERS / Dry the capers by patting with a paper towel. Place 1 cm (½ inch) olive oil in the smallest saucepan you can find so you'll use as little oil as possible. Heat until the oil begins to move on its surface. Test by adding a caper. If it sizzles and fries, the oil's hot enough. Add the capers in two batches, frying for 30 seconds, then remove with a slotted spoon to a plate lined with paper towel. These will last for a few days on paper towel in a covered container.

TO ASSEMBLE / Preheat the oven to 220°C (425°F). Take the sheet of pizza and if the dough has risen excessively, press down gently with the tips of your fingers to make small indentations. Distribute the mozzarella on top of the dough as evenly as possible. Sprinkle with the parmesan and oregano. Evenly spread about three-quarters of the cooked broccoli on top and bake in the oven for 25 minutes. If the teglia is browning more on one side, your oven is not even and the tray may need to be turned. Once cooked, remove from the oven and let cool a little. Place on a serving plate as a large piece or cut into individual tiles. Distribute the anchovies, then the fried capers, confit tomatoes and finally the caper leaves on top. Finish with extra virgin olive oil.

Serves 6–8

Prosciutto and bufala

This has become a modern classic with many pizzerie offering their own version. Once again, it's the quality of the ingredients that set the best apart. My preference is for 24 month-aged Prosciutto di Parma. The prosciutto is always best sliced at the last minute.

250 g (9 oz) ball of basic pizza dough (see pages 18–21), shaped (see pages 22–25)

120 g (4¼ oz) buffalo mozzarella
1 tablespoon grated parmesan cheese
35 g (1¼ oz/1 cup) rocket (arugula), thick stems removed
6–8 slices of Prosciutto di Parma
1 tablespoon extra virgin olive oil

ROAST CHERRY TOMATOES

1 kg (2 lb 4 oz) cherry or small roma (plum) tomatoes
2 tablespoons extra virgin olive oil
Sea salt and freshly ground black pepper

FOR THE ROAST CHERRY TOMATOES / Preheat the oven to 170°C (340°F). Prepare the tomatoes by slicing them in half and place, cut side up, on a baking tray. Drizzle with the olive oil, salt and pepper and roast for about 15 minutes. Remove and let them cool before using. Any leftover tomatoes can be kept in the refrigerator for up to 5 days.

TO ASSEMBLE / Place a large tile in your oven for the pizza, then turn the oven up to preheat to full heat (without using any fan-forced function) for at least 20 minutes (see page 31). Cut the mozzarella into 1 cm (½ inch) cubes and scatter evenly, here and there, to top the shaped pizza base, leaving the edges clear to about 3–4 cm (1½ inches). Scatter the parmesan on top and then evenly distribute 18 of the roast cherry tomato halves over the top. Place the pizza in the oven for 3–5 minutes until cooked, turning to get an even colour. Once out, scatter the rocket leaves over, arrange the prosciutto slices evenly and drizzle with olive oil.

Makes one 30 cm (12 inch) pizza

OPPOSITE / Preparing the ancient pizza oven. **THIS PAGE** / Harvesting San Marzano tomatoes by hand.

Rio – banana and macadamia sweet calzone

This is a filled dessert pizza devised by Pizzaperta chef Gianluca Donzelli to commemorate the Brazil leg of the World Surf League: The Rio Pro.

250 g (9 oz) ball of basic pizza dough (see pages 18–21), shaped as you would a normal round pizza (see pages 22–25)

40 g (1½ oz/¼ cup) ricotta cheese
50 g (1¾ oz/⅓ cup) 70% cocoa dark chocolate buttons
1 large banana, halved lengthways
1 tablespoon guava jam
1 tablespoon icing (confectioners') sugar, for dusting
1 tablespoon amarena cherries or other berry coulis

MACADAMIA BRITTLE
170 g (6 oz/1⅓ cups) shelled, unsalted macadamia pieces
270 g (9½ oz/1¼ cups) sugar
60 ml (2 fl oz/¼ cup) water
60 ml (2 fl oz/¼ cup) light corn syrup
35 g (1¼ oz/2 tablespoons) unsalted butter
½ teaspoon baking powder
Pinch of sea salt

FOR THE MACADAMIA BRITTLE / Place the shelled, unsalted macadamias on a baking tray and roast in a 180°C (350°F) oven for 10–12 minutes. Allow the nuts to cool. In a saucepan combine the sugar, water, corn syrup and butter. Cook over a medium heat until the mixture is a light caramel colour. Remove from the heat and quickly whisk in the baking powder, salt and the macadamia nuts. With a buttered spatula, spread the mixture quickly onto a non-stick baking sheet. Cool completely. Break into shards or grind in a mortar and pestle or food processor to make praline. The brittle can be stored in an airtight container between sheets of baking paper for up to 2 weeks.

TO ASSEMBLE / Place a large tile in your oven for the pizza, then preheat to full heat (without using any fan-forced function) for at least 20 minutes (see page 31). Spread the ricotta on one half of the dough circle, remembering that it will be folded over and sealed into a crescent shape. Scatter the buttons over the ricotta, then place the two banana halves on top. Fold the dough over the filling, forming a crescent shape, and seal by pinching the edge gently. Place the pizza in the oven for 3–5 minutes until cooked, turning to get an even colour. Once cooked, remove from the oven and place on a chopping board. Cut into four pieces. Place on a serving plate. Put a little guava jam on top of each piece, dust with icing sugar, scatter over 1 tablespoon of the crushed macadamia brittle and finish by drizzling on the berry coulis.

Serves 4

Struffoli

This festive Neapolitan Christmas treat is easy to make at any time of year. It's usually formed as little balls, but these irregular shapes are easier to eat with your fingers.

250 g (9 oz) ball of basic pizza
  dough (see pages 18–21)

500 ml (17 fl oz/2 cups) extra virgin
  olive oil, for frying
175 g (6 oz/½ cup) honey
1 tablespoon grated lemon zest
1 tablespoon grated orange zest
2 tablespoons white sugar confetti
1 tablespoon chopped candied
  cedro (citron)

TO ASSEMBLE / Roll the dough into a long sausage – about 2 cm (¾ inch) thick – on a lightly floured work surface and cut into around 12 pieces, each about 5 cm (2 inches) long. Heat the olive oil in a pot or deep-fryer to 175°C (350°F). Once at that temperature, place the dough pieces carefully in one at a time and fry until crisp and golden. They may need to be turned or moved. Remove with a slotted spoon or strainer and drain on paper towel.

While the struffoli are draining, heat the honey over a medium heat, in a small saucepan, until it's very liquid and runny. Using a spoon, drizzle the honey over the struffoli to coat them well. Sprinkle with lemon and orange zest and top with the sugar confetti and candied cedro.

Serves 4

Pillow of dreams

Italians love their Nutella. It's a treat given to them in their childhood and many continue this love affair when they become adults. Nutella is now famous throughout the world, but its origins begin with Italian pastry maker, Pietro Ferrero, who created a chocolate bar cut with high-quality Piemontese hazelnut paste. That was in 1946 when chocolate was in short supply post-war. It became an instant success. Many loved having bread and chocolate for breakfast, so in 1951 a version with a creamy, spreadable consistency was invented called Supercrema. It was Pietro's son Michele who rebranded it as Nutella in 1963 and it is now enjoyed by millions of people all over the world. This is Pizzaperta's version of a Nutella pizza. When our chef, Gianluca Donzelli, created it he said it was 'like a dream'. 'A pillow of dreams,' I said. Indeed it is.

250 g (9 oz) ball of basic pizza
   dough (see pages 18–21), shaped
   as you would a normal round pizza,
   but make it larger by not leaving
   a cornice on the edge
   (see pages 22–25)

4 tablespoons Nutella
2 tablespoons flaked almonds
Icing (confectioners') sugar, for dusting
1 scoop of vanilla gelato
2 strawberries, halved
1 tablespoon thinly sliced fresh mint
   leaves
1 sprig of fresh mint

TO ASSEMBLE / Place a large tile in your oven for the pizza, then preheat to full heat (without using any fan-forced function) for at least 20 minutes (see page 31). Cut the pizza base into as large a square as possible. Place a tablespoon of Nutella halfway between each corner and the middle of the square. Scatter the flaked almonds on top of each tablespoon of Nutella. Fold each of the corners of the dough into the centre over the filling, forming a smaller square, and seal by pinching the edges gently where the folds meet. Place the pizza in the oven for 3–5 minutes until cooked, turning to get an even colour. Once cooked, remove from the oven and place on a board. Sprinkle with a light dusting of icing sugar. Place on a serving plate. Add a scoop of vanilla gelato in the middle, a strawberry half in each corner and scatter the sliced mint on top. Finish with a mint sprig on the gelato.

Serves 4

Index

Published in 2018 by Murdoch Books, an imprint of Allen & Unwin
This book is an abridged version of *New Pizza*, published by Murdoch Books 2017

Murdoch Books Australia
83 Alexander Street, Crows Nest NSW 2065
Phone: +61 (0)2 8425 0100
murdochbooks.com.au
info@murdochbooks.com.au

Murdoch Books UK
Ormond House, 26–27 Boswell Street
London WC1N 3JZ
Phone: +44 (0) 20 8785 5995
murdochbooks.co.uk
info@murdochbooks.co.uk

For corporate orders and custom publishing contact our business development team
at salesenquiries@murdochbooks.com.au

Publisher: Corinne Roberts
Design Manager: Hugh Ford
Editorial Manager: Jane Price
Editors: Kay Halsey and Justin Wolfers
Photographer: Bree Hutchins (except pages 32, 33 and 135 by Gustarosso Foto)
Design Concept: Frost*collective, Sydney
Production Director: Lou Playfair

Text © Stefano Manfredi 2017
Design © Murdoch Books 2017
Photography © Bree Hutchins 2017

ISBN 978 1 76063 196 3 Australia
ISBN 978 1 76063 442 1 UK

A cataloguing-in-publication entry is available from the catalogue
of the National Library of Australia at nla.gov.au
A catalogue record for this book is available from the British Library

Colour reproduction by Splitting Image Colour Studio Pty Ltd, Clayton, Victoria
Printed by Hang Tai Printing Company Ltd, China

MEASURES GUIDE: We have used 20 ml (4 teaspoon) tablespoon measures. If you are using a 15 ml
(3 teaspoon) tablespoon add an extra teaspoon of the ingredient for each tablespoon specified.